The Open University

Social Sciences: a third level course
Regional analysis and development III

The Micro Approach –
economic and social surfaces

Unit 9 Human migration

Unit 10 The consequences of labour migration

Prepared for the course team by Gareth Lewis
Lecturer in Geography, Leicester University

Unit 11 Economic complexes

Prepared for the course team by Charles Choguill
Lecturer in Town and Regional Planning, Sheffield University

The Open University

The Open University Press
Walton Hall, Milton Keynes

First published 1974

Designed by the Media Development Group of the Open University.

Printed in Great Britain by
COES THE PRINTERS LIMITED
RUSTINGTON SUSSEX

ISBN 0 335 04898 6

This text forms part of an Open University course. The complete list of units in the course appears at the end of this text.

For general availability of supporting material referred to in this text, please write to the Director of Marketing, The Open University, P.O. Box 81, Walton Hall, Milton Keynes MK7 6AT.

Further information on Open University courses may be obtained from the Admissions Office, The Open University, P.O. Box 48, Walton Hall, Milton Keynes, MK7 6AB.

1.2

Unit 9
Human migration

Prepared by Gareth Lewis

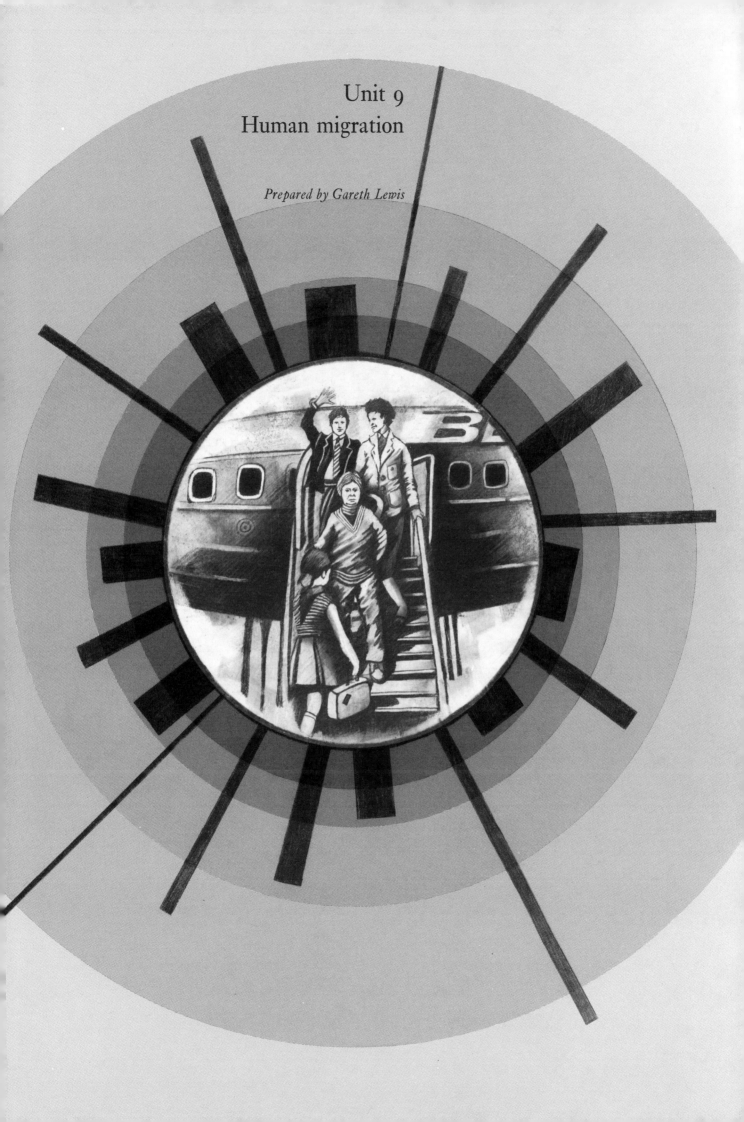

Contents

		Page
1	Introduction	7
2	Operational definitions	8
2.1	What is migration?	8
2.2	Concepts in migration studies	8
2.3	A general typology of migration	9
3	Methods of deriving migration data	10
4	A systems approach	11
5	The process of migration	13
5.1	Why do people migrate?	14
5.1.1	Push-pull factors	14
5.1.2	Formal models	14
5.1.3	Personal motivation	15
5.1.4	Obstacles to migration	17
5.2	Where do people migrate to?	17
5.3	Who are the migrants?	20
5.4	How do people decide to migrate?	22
6	Patterns of migration	24
6.1	Ghana	24
6.2	The United States	25
6.3	Discussion	25
6.4	Conclusion	26
	Self-assessment questions	26
	References	28

1 Introduction

Although the migration of people was mentioned briefly in Units 6 and 7, its importance for regional development necessitates an examination in its own right. Since Unit 6 discussed the nature of migration at the regional level, this Unit will focus its attention at the micro – or surface scale. However, much of the discussion presented will have relevance to the regional framework of approach.

Human migration, or the movement of individuals and groups from one home location to another, has been taking place since the origins of man. During recorded history migration has not only increased in volume but has also involved steadily lengthening distances. It is usual to divide the field of migration into two:

1   International migration, or the movement of people between nations, and

2   Internal migration, or the movement of people within a nation.

Since the movement of people between nation-states is now relatively restricted, this unit will focus its attention largely upon migration within national boundaries.

Migration is a major agent of social change, since it can be viewed as an independent as well as a dependent variable in the examination of change (see Unit 4 p 56). Within the context of the surface concept such changes can be conceived in terms of 'hills' of increasing population and 'valleys' of declining population. It is now well recognized that migration is the most important single factor explaining why the population of one part of a demographic surface grows faster than another. This is due to the fact that differences in birth-rates and death-rates between various parts of the surface are often rather small in comparison with differences in migration rates. In addition, if such migratory movements are selective of individuals with particular economic or social attributes, then they will give rise to differences in the socio-economic composition of different parts of the demographic surface

With the increasing amount and diversity of migration throughout the world, there has been a corresponding increase in the desire and necessity to identify and explain such movements. From the point of view of regional development four reasons can be suggested why an understanding of the process and the identification of the patterns of migration is important:

(a) It is necessary to predict population change of specific areas or regions. It is being increasingly recognized that migration is the critical variable in economic development, as well as population growth, at a regional level. With a better understanding of the migration process more accurate prediction would ensue, and hence better-informed regional economic policies.

(b) It is necessary to identify and explain the reasons why employees, and even employers, move from one region to another. With knowledge of such factors, economists and regional analysts would be better able to channel development into desired locations and regions.

(c) How and why people move is of crucial importance in any understanding of the social patterning of society and its changing form, both at an urban and regional level. We have already indicated the significance of migration as an agent of social change.

(d) It is necessary to identify and explain why families change their place of residence. With such knowledge those concerned with housing, both at an urban and at regional level, will be in a better position not only to guide private and public housing schemes but also to reduce the socio-economic problems caused by haphazard residential developments.

The purpose of this unit, therefore, is to elucidate the components of the migration process and its spatial manifestation. Briefly, the unit is divided into four parts. First, a series of basic concepts and definitions will be presented; second, the components of the migration process will be identified, within the context of a simple migration system; third, the nature of each component will be analysed within a decision-making framework, and fourth, the patterns resulting from the process of migration will be outlined, with special reference to Ghana and the United States.

2 Operational definitions

Why should we need to define migration once again, when so many definitions already exist? Any review of migration literature will quickly reveal that there are a number of false or inadequate conceptions concerning the nature of migration, and these have led to unsatisfactory definitions of the phenomenon. These inadequate definitions have given rise to a series of weakly-developed typologies of the patterns of migration.

2.1 What is migration?

The term 'migration' seems clearest when defined in the light of the demographic balancing equation:

$$P_t = P_o + B - D + I - O$$

where

P_t = population at the close of the interval

P_o = population at the beginning of the interval

D = number of deaths in the interval

B = number of births in the interval

O = the number of out-migrants in the interval

I = the number of in-migrants in the interval.

Clearly a 'migrant' is a person entering or leaving a place or region by means other than birth or death, and the total *gross* or *net* increments caused by such entrances (in-migration) or departures (out-migration) constitute 'migration'.

However, many have argued that such a definition of migration is too narrowly conceived, since migration involves a whole series of dimensions additional to that of a change of residence. Two often-quoted definitions give us a clue as to the nature of these additional dimensions: 'We define migration as the physical transition of an individual or a group from one society to another. This transition usually involves abandoning one social setting and entering another and different one' (Eisenstadt 1954 p 1). 'Migration is defined ... as the movements (involving change of permanent residence) from one country to another which take place through the volition of the individuals or families concerned' (Thomas 1959 p 510).

The two additional dimensions revealed by these quotations are, firstly, that migration is a form of motivated behaviour and, secondly, that migration causes changes in the interactional system of the people involved. Such interactional changes involve a weakening of social and cultural attachments with the place of origin, and the creation of new ties and values in the place of destination. The degree to which the new values are accepted becomes a major determinant of the migrant's rate of assimilation into the new community. Since migration is an act of volition it implies decision-making, which in turn depends on some underlying criteria; these criteria will involve a hierarchy of values. A more appropriate definition of migration for the purpose of this unit, then, which incorporates these two dimensions, is that suggested by Mangalam:

Migration is a relatively permanent moving away of a collectivity, called migrants, from one geographical location to another, preceded by decision-making on the part of the migrants on the basis of a hierarchically ordered set of values or valued ends and resulting in changes in the interactional system of the migrants (Mangalam 1968 p 11).

2.2 Concepts in migration studies

Within the field of migration there are a number of operational concepts which are in regular use; the manner in which they are defined has crucial repercussions for the findings of particular studies. For example, the proportion of individuals classified as migrants will depend to a considerable extent upon the size and shape of the areal unit used in the analysis. The greater the size of the areal unit, the fewer will be the

8

movers defined as migrants. In addition, it is necessary to specify the interval of time over which migration is to be observed. The longer the interval, the smaller will be the size of the average annual number of migrants, because a significant proportion of persons who migrate return to their original place of residence. Migratory movements take place at different frequencies both in time and space, and their rates may be calculated for out- and in-migrations, both net and gross.

2.3 A general typology of migration

In order to simplify the complexities of the migration process numerous attempts have been made to classify the movements of people into various types. By far the most famous is Peterson's *General Typology of Migration* (1958), which has been summarized in Table 1. Such migration types, according to Peterson, are the result

Table 1   A General Typology of Migration

Relation	Migratory force	Class of Migration	Type of Migration Conservative	Innovating
Nature and man	Ecological push	Primitive	{ Wandering { Ranging	Flight from the land
State (or equivalent) and man	Migration policy	{ Forced { Impelled	{ Displacement { Flight	{ Slave trade { Coolie trade
Man and his norms	Higher aspirations	Free	Group	Pioneer
Collective behaviour	Social momentum	Mass	Settlement	Urbanization

Source: Peterson (1958)

of differential forces operating within society and resulting in differential migratory responses. This unit has been conceived within the context of individual and collective behaviour (*cf.* 'Man and his norms' and 'Collective behaviour', Table 1). However, Cavalli-Sforza's *Morphological Classification of Human Movements* (1962), and its later adaptation by Roseman (1971), is a more meaningful typology of migration, since it is conceived within the overall context of human movements.

Figure 1a   Reciprocal Movement   Figure 1b   Total Displacement Migration

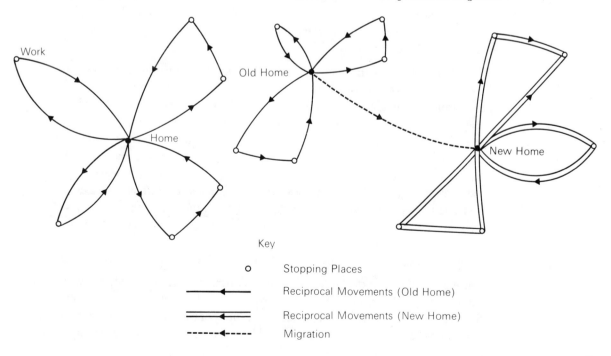

Key

o   Stopping Places

←   Reciprocal Movements (Old Home)

⇐   Reciprocal Movements (New Home)

-----←-----   Migration

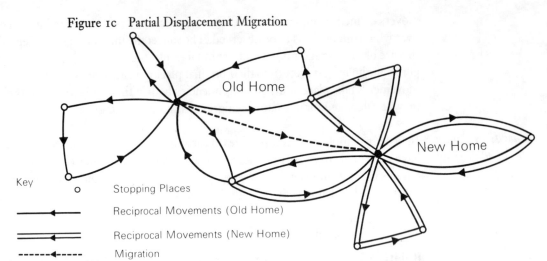

Figure 1c   Partial Displacement Migration

Old Home

New Home

Key
○   Stopping Places
────◄────   Reciprocal Movements (Old Home)
════◄════   Reciprocal Movements (New Home)
------◄----- Migration

Source of Figures 1a–c: based on Roseman (1971)

Such a classification argues that human movements may be classified into two broad categories. The first is what is called *Reciprocal Movements* of people (Figure 1a). These begin at the home, proceed to one or more alternative locations, and return to the home. Such places include the work-place, entertainment centres, shopping places, homes of friends and relatives, and so on. The second category consists of *Migratory Movements*, which are distinguished from the first in that they are predominantly uni-directional and permanent. Basically, they represent the removal of the centre of gravity of the Reciprocal Movements, the home, to a new location. With regard to these movements, two forms of migration may be identified. The first includes residential changes whereby a completely new Reciprocal Movement cycle is created by a movement to a new area. This is called *Total Displacement Migration* (Figure 1b). The second involves migration that displaces only part of the Reciprocal Movement cycle: although the location of the home changes, the locations of some of the other activity nodes still remain the same. This is called *Partial Displacement Migration* (Figure 1c). As we shall see later in this unit, such a distinction has considerable significance for an understanding of the complexities of the migration process. In addition, Total and Partial Displacement Migration may be conceived as being broadly analogous to inter-regional and intra-urban (or rural) migration respectively.

3   Methods of deriving migration data

Basically, there are two methods of obtaining data on internal migration: *direct* methods, or a simple count of individuals who move across a defined boundary within a given time-period; and *indirect* methods, or the estimation of migrants from vital-rates tables.

To obtain migration data by means of the direct method, the most common source is the *national census*, although in Britain it was not until 1961 that questions on migration were first inserted. Unfortunately, only moves which had occurred in the year, or the whole five-year period, preceding census-taking day were recorded. The most significant weakness of such a source is the void thus created by the time-interval between successive censuses. However, this difficulty can be overcome if a country has a law, as Scandinavian countries do, which requires each person who changes his residence to report the fact to the local council. *National registration* tables, derived from such reports, provide a detailed dossier on the number and characteristics of migrants, though, unfortunately, not all countries have such a scheme. Despite their restricted nature, both of these methods (which can be supplemented by *sample surveys*) do provide a valuable insight into the complexities of the migration process.

The most common form of indirect method of measurement is to compare, within the national census, a person's place of birth with his residence at the time of enumeration. Such *place-of-birth statistics* give useful indications of the direction of migration flows. If statistics on births and deaths are available, it is possible to estimate net migration by subtracting reproductive population change from total change between two successive censuses. More simply the *vital statistics* can be expressed by the equation:

$$M = (P_t - P_o) - (B - D)$$

where M is the net migration during the inter-censal period

P_t and P_o are the population at the end and beginning, respectively, of the inter-censal period

B and D are the number of births and deaths, respectively, during the inter-censal period.

A similar approach is adopted by the often-used *survival ratio* method. This estimates the number of individuals at one census period who would still be alive and resident in the same location at the succeeding census on the assumption of no migration. The number of migrants is then calculated by subtracting the estimated number of people who would still be alive from the actual census count at the second census. The hypothetical estimate is obtained by multiplying each age-group of the first census by a net 'survival ratio', which is a statistical estimate of the proportion of that age-group who will still be alive at the next census:

$$M_i = P_t - P_{os}$$

where M_i is the number of migrants

P_t and P_{os} are the population according to age-groups at the end and beginning, respectively, of the inter-censal period

s is the estimate of the number in the age-group who will survive from the first census to the second.

Finally, it should be noted that all three indirect methods of migration estimation can indicate only gross migration patterns for large areal units.

4 A systems approach

In the past, the process of migration has too often been viewed as a uni-linear, cause-effect type of movement. Such an approach is exceedingly restrictive and fails to emphasize that all components within the migration process are inter-related. A change in the nature of one component can have an effect upon all the others. Such inter-relationships can be more easily understood if we conceive of migration as a system. Simply, a system is a complex of interacting elements, together with their attributes and relationships. Migration is then viewed as a circular, inter-dependent and self-modifying system in which the effects of changes in one part have a ripple effect throughout the whole system. By viewing migration as a system it is possible to identify the interacting elements, their attributes and their relationships.

In order to outline the components of such a migration system we shall present in the succeeding paragraphs a brief summary of the arguments contained in Mabogunje's paper 'A systems approach to rural-urban migration' (1970). Although Mabogunje was concerned with rural-urban migration in Africa, his analysis of the process in systems language has wider relevance. Figure 2 is an outline of the rural-urban migration process in Africa. The *environment* of such a migration system is one in which the rural communities are experiencing a break-up of their isolation and self-sufficiency. The main agent of such change is economic development. In the majority of the African states this was initiated by the colonial administrations and, in recent years, further reinforced by the activities of the newly independent régimes. The rural economy is being increasingly integrated into the national economy, with resulting changes in the countryside in wage and price levels and in levels of expectation and demand. The villager has become more aware of the greater range of opportunities the cities provide. This environment, then, determines the extent and nature of the migration.

A migration system is made up of three basic *elements*. First, there is the potential

Figure 2   A rural–urban migration system

ENVIRONMENT
Economic Conditions—Wages, Prices, Consumer Preferences,
Degrees of Commercialization and Industrial Development

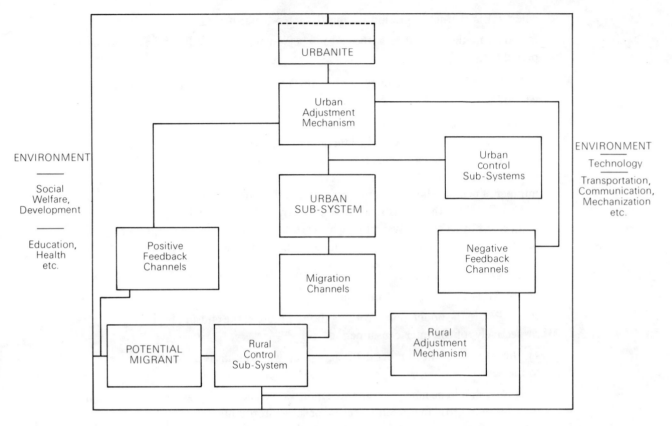

ENVIRONMENT

Social
Welfare,
Development

Education,
Health
etc.

ENVIRONMENT

Technology

Transportation,
Communication,
Mechanization
etc.

ENVIRONMENT

Governmental Policies, Agricultural Practices,
Marketing Organizations, Population Movement etc.

Source: Mabogunje (1970)

The term sub-system used in the above diagram can be defined as the interrelationship between a set of
elements which together form an identifiable unit despite a certain amount of influence from outside
elements; the term system is normally used for cases in which there is no, or very little, external influence.

migrant, who is encouraged to leave the rural village by stimuli from the
environment. Second, there are the various institutions – the control sub-systems –
which determine the level of flow within the system: in the context of rural–urban
migration the two most important are the rural and urban control sub-systems. In the
rural area the nuclear and extended family, and the local community, by means of
the various activities which it sponsors, can act both in a positive and negative way in
determining the volume of migration. On the other hand, the urban control
sub-system determines, by means of occupational and residential opportunities,
the degree of assimilation into the urban environment. Third, there are the various
social, economic and political forces, or adjustment mechanisms, which play a
significant role in the process of a migrant's transformation. The act of migration
sets in motion a series of adjustments both in the village and the city. Within the
rural area it involves a loss of one productive unit, as well as one member of family
and community life, whilst in the city the migrant is incorporated into a new
situation more relevant to his needs.

All systems contain a driving force, or *energy*, which in the case of the rural–urban
migration system can be equated with the stimuli to move acting on the rural
individual. This involves, not only a recognition of such stimuli themselves, but also
the differential responses of rural dwellers to them. Mabogunje argues that in the case
of Africa the stimulus to migrate is 'related to the degree of the integration of the rural

economy into the national economy, to the degree of awareness of opportunities outside of the rural areas, and to the nature of the social and economic expectations held by the rural population' (Mabogunje 1970 p 14). In systems language this is what is called *potential energy*; with movement, it is translated into *kinetic energy*. The actual migration raises questions of the cost and direction of the movement, since these determine the channels and patterns of the migration.

A rural dweller's role in the system does not end with his migration to the city, because by means of a feedback of information to his original village he can modify the system's behaviour. Without the feedback, the distribution of migrants from a village will become, over time, proportional to the size of the city in question. In other words, the system has no order or organization, and can be said to be in a state of *maximum entropy* (or disorder), that is, in the most unpredictable state. When the rural migrant maintains contact with his home, the feedback information about life in the city can be either negative or positive. In the former case the migration to the city will slow down to a trickle, while in the latter a regular migration from particular villages to particular cities will be encouraged. Therefore, the existence of information in the system tends to encourage either a decrease in the level of entropy (or disorder) or an increase in negative entropy.

Although the migration system presented here is one designed specifically to aid an understanding of rural-to-urban migration in Africa, it does provide additional and broader insight into the migration process in general. Migration is conceived as a circular process in which the effects of changes in one part can be traced through the whole system. In addition, such a system emphasizes the point that we should be concerned, not only with why people migrate, but with all the implications and ramifications of the process. Basically, six questions are raised by such a migration system to which we need to seek answers:

1 Why do people migrate?

2 Where do people migrate to?

3 Who are the migrants?

4 How do people decide to migrate?

5 What changes do migrants undergo during the process?

6 What effects does migration have on the society of origin and the society of destination of the migrants?

The first four of these questions will be discussed in the next section of this unit, and the last two in Unit 10.

5 The process of migration

Unlike birth and death, migration has no physiological component; rather, it is a response by humans to a series of economic, social and political stimuli within the environment. According to Wolpert (1965) such stimuli take the form of the *attractiveness* of a location (or its *place utility*) for specific purposes (see Course Reader). The action of migration can be motivated by changes either in a person's value system or within the environment. If, as a result of these changes, the person becomes dissatisfied with his home location, then a desire to migrate will be generated. The strength of the desire to migrate, and whether it is fulfilled or not, will vary according to the needs of the individual, the constraints upon him and the strength of the dissatisfaction, and will also vary at successive stages of the life-cycle. The place to which an individual finally migrates will be determined, not only by the *locational structure of opportunities*, but also by the *movement cost* involved. However, knowledge of such opportunities will not be perfect, since it will be biased by an individual's *activity space* (for example, the location of work, leisure, cultural activities, etc.) and by his *indirect contact space* (for example, the location of friends, relatives, the mass media, etc.).

| 5.1 | *Why do people migrate?* | People's reasons for migrating can be explained only in terms of the relative attractiveness of different locations, or differential place utilities. |

| 5.1.1 | *Push-pull factors* | Herberle (1938) has argued that there is a series of forces which encourage an individual to leave one place (push) and attract him to another (pull). Bogue has succinctly summarized these 'push-pull' forces as follows: |

Push factors

1 Decline in a national resource or in the prices paid for it; decreased demand for a particular product or the services of a particular industry; exhaustion of mines, timber or agricultural resources.

2 Loss of employment resulting from being discharged for incompetence, from a decline in need for a particular activity, or from mechanization or automation of tasks previously performed by more labour-intensive procedures.

3 Oppressive or repressive discriminatory treatment because of political, religious or ethnic origins or membership.

4 Alienation from a community because one no longer subscribes to prevailing beliefs, actions, or modes of behaviour either within one's family or within the community.

5 Retreat from a community because it offers few or no opportunities for personal development, employment or marriage.

6 Retreat from a community because of catastrophe – floods, fire, drought, earthquake or epidemic.

Pull factors

1 Superior opportunities for employment in one's occupation or opportunities to enter a preferred occupation.

2 Opportunities to earn a larger income.

3 Opportunities to obtain desired specialized education or training such as a college education.

4 Preferable environment and living conditions – climate, housing, schools, other community facilities.

5 Dependency – movement of other persons to whom one is related or betrothed, such as the movement of dependants with a bread-winner or migration of a bride to join her husband.

6 Lure of new or different activities, environment, or people, such as the cultural, intellectual, or recreational activities of a large metropolis for rural and small-town residence (Bogue 1969 pp 753–4).

A careful inspection of these 'push-pull' factors reveals the existence of two undifferentiated sets of forces. On the one hand, there are stimuli to migrate created by changes within the environment, and on the other, changes in the personal motives of the individual.

Clearly such factors can be conceived within the context of a surface, a 'high' in one part and a 'low' in another. Changes in the environment, for example, can be interpreted as prolonged disequilibria of particular kinds in various parts of the surface. The most easily recognisable disequilibrium is that created by variations in economic opportunities. Often migration streams in this respect have been explained in terms of movements from areas of unemployment to ones with greater employment opportunities.

Two methods can be devised to test the existence of such factors
(a) aggregate formal models and (b) studies of personal motivations.

| 5.1.2 | *Formal models* | The majority of the formal models here emphasized the significance of the economic motive in determining migration, and conceptually the Lowry model appears to |

be the most satisfactory. This model can be represented by the equation:

$$M_{ij} = K \left[\frac{U_i}{U_j} \cdot \frac{W_j}{W_i} \cdot \frac{L_i L_j}{D_{ij}} \right] E_{ij}$$

where M_{ij} = numbers of migrants from area i to area j

L_i, L_j = numbers of persons in non-agricultural employment in i and j respectively

U_i, U_j = unemployment as a percentage of the number in non-agricultural employment in i and j respectively

W_i, W_j = hourly manufacturing wage in i and j respectively

D_{ij} = straight-line distance separating i and j

E_{ij} = error term

K = a constant (Lowry 1966).

The value of the Lowry Model lies not only in its identification of a gradient of opportunities across a surface but also the ease with which it can be adapted for empirical investigation. Andrei Rogers (1968), for example, in a study of inter-county migration in California made some modification to the variables in order to reflect the significant role of agriculture in a number of the counties in California. The modifications were:

L_i, L_j = number of persons in the civilian labour force in county i and county j respectively

U_i, U_j = unemployment as a percentage of the civilian labour force in i and j respectively

D_{ij} = road mileage separating the major county seats in i and j.

Using a regression analysis, Rogers was able to claim that over ninety per cent of the variation in the migration pattern in California was accounted for by the seven variables, of which four were significantly different from zero at five-per-cent confidence level. Five of the seven variables had the signs which one would have expected. The coefficients of unemployment rates in i and j should, on *a priori* grounds, have been positive and negative respectively, but, surprisingly, the analysis revealed a reversal of the signs and neither were statistically significant. Rogers found this finding difficult to explain, and argued that unemployment should therefore be left out of the model.

In contrast, Oliver (1964), in a study of inter-regional migration in England and Wales between 1951 and 1961, argued that the most striking feature shown by his data was the loss of people through migration from regions with high unemployment and the gain by regions with high employment-opportunities. A similar, but even more striking, pattern was that identified by Allan Rodgers (1970) in Italy. Between 1951 and 1961 the majority of the 1.8 million southern Italians who left their places of origin migrated to the booming northern industrial cities of Rome, Turin, Milan and Genoa.

5.1.3 *Personal motivation*

In both the Lowry model and the empirical studies cited above the apparent reason why the migration took place was inferred from the patterns revealed and the attributes of the areas involved. The *actual* reasons why people migrate, however, can only be derived from detailed surveys in the field. Bearing in mind the difficulties of asking questions without biasing the responses, we can derive some idea as to the nature of people's motives in migrating by reference to four case-studies:

1 Sjastaad in 1962 carried out a cost-benefit analysis to reveal the relative order of factors generating migration. Within the study migration was regarded as an investment activity which required a cost to be incurred and a return to be produced. Such costs included both financial costs, such as 'opportunities forgone' and costs incurred in moving the family and its effects, and social costs, which involved an

estimate of the loss in leaving the home environment, friends, and relatives. Migration was most likely to occur when the benefits were greater than the costs. Although Sjastaad concluded that the monetary factor was the most significant motive in the migration process, he did emphasize that the social factor had been underestimated in a number of previous studies.

2 Pourcher (1963), in a survey made in 1961 of the inhabitants of Greater Paris, aged 21–60 and born in the provinces, gave seven major reasons for moves into the capital:

(a) Wish for promotion   29%
(b) Assigned, nominated transfer   16%
(c) Without work or means of subsistence in provinces   14%
(d) Marriage, and motives independent of mover (children accompanying
       parents, etc).   14%
(e) Family and housing reasons   12%
(f) Education   9%
(g) Desire for change   6%

3 Lewis (1969), in a study of rural migration in the Welsh Borderland between 1958 and 1968, identified five major categories of migration motives for both in- and out-migrants. Table 2 is a summary of the migrants' responses, and the reader's attention is drawn to the variation in the proportions of the motives of those moving into and those moving out of the region.

Table 2   Motives for migrating in the Welsh Borderland, 1958–68

Motive	Out-migrants %	In-migrants %
Occupational	32	13
Income	29	9
Social	19	36
Community	12	18
Personal	8	24

Source: Lewis (1969)

4 Rossi, in his classic study of residential mobility in Philadelphia (1965), concluded that employment and income aspirations played only a small part in determining the level of *intra-urban* migration. He differentiated the motives for moving into those relating to the former home area, and those relating to the choice of migration destination (*cf.* Wolpert 1965). The decision to leave the former home was based upon such factors as marriage, divorce, employment, eviction, even the demolition of the dwelling, whilst those with a choice of moving or staying migrated in search of more space, better neighbourhoods and cheaper rents.

Although the first three surveys cited emphasize the role of the economic motive, particularly employment, in determining migration levels, they do also indicate the increasing significance of social factors, particular the family and housing. Surprisingly, in a conclusion to a sample survey of labour mobility in England and Wales, Harris and Clausen (1966) have gone a step further by claiming that wages and employment played only a minor role in migration decision-making. However, such a statement may not be as controversial as it seems, when it is recalled that the majority of migrations occur over short distances. As shown by Rossi in an urban area and Lewis in a rural area, such migrations are overwhelmingly determined by factors of a social nature. Therefore, it may be tentatively claimed that:

1 economic factors, such as wages and employment, tend to be of greater significance

in determining Total Displacement (or long-distance) Migration, whereas social motives, such as housing and family, are of greater relevance in explaining Partial Displacement (or short-distance) Migration; and

2 the intensity of an out-migration will tend to vary with the strength of attractive 'pulls' from other places and, conversely, with expulsive 'pushes' from the home area itself.

5.1.4 Obstacles to migration

Finally, it is false to assume that, whenever the flow of migration is small, all the needs of people are being satisfied. It is now well established that there exist a number of forces which can prevent an individual from migrating, even when there are high levels of dissatisfaction. Three examples will illustrate this point:

(a) Zachariah (1964) has shown that many illiterate villagers in India find it difficult to move from conditions which threaten them with starvation because they lack skills and opportunities for other employment in another rural area or in the cities.

(b) Davies (1966) has argued that many general practitioners in England and Wales would prefer to be in practice in the south-east region. Between 1953 and 1957 the number of doctors applying for a vacancy in practices of 2,000 or more patients in the north of England averaged 27, whereas similar practices in southern England received on average 53 applications. This effectively proves the spatial preferences of doctors for the south, and since the economic motive, financial gain, is standardized, other factors are needed to explain the pattern. In other words, doctors' migration desires are being constrained by an insufficiency of opportunities in the south, and are thus creating a latent migration potential of doctors in the remaining regions.

(c) Lewis (1969) has shown that over twenty-one per cent of rural dwellers in the Welsh Borderland wish to migrate. However, such potential migrants are frustrated in achieving their desires by a number of factors, including (in descending order of importance): a lack of suitable alternative employment, strong family ties, shortages of suitable housing elsewhere, and the high cost of moving.

These three examples clearly emphasize the existence of a considerable degree of *latent migration potential* within different societies, and the significance of both social and economic obstacles in the creation of it.

5.2 Where do people migrate to?

An explanation of where a migrant is most likely to move to can only be achieved by reference to the locational structure of available opportunities and the degree to which the migrant is constrained by such factors as movement costs. Such a framework was identified as long ago as the 1880s by E. G. Ravenstein in his 'Laws of Migration'. Using the birthplace statistics contained in the 1881 census of England and Wales, Ravenstein suggested the following migration trends:

1 We have already proved that the great body of our migrants only proceed a short distance and that there takes place consequently a universal shifting or displacement of the population, which produces 'currents of migration' setting in the direction of the great centres of commerce and industry which absorb the migrants.

2 It is the natural outcome of this movement of migration limited in range, but universal throughout the country, that the processes of absorption go on in the following manner: the inhabitants of a country immediately surrounding a town of rapid growth, flock to it; the gaps thus left by the rural population are filled up by the migrants from more remote districts, until the attractive force of one of our rapidly growing cities makes its influence felt, step by step, to the most remote corner of the Kingdom. Migrants enumerated in a certain centre of absorption will consequently grow less with the distance proportionately to the native population which furnishes them . . . .

3 The process of dispersion is the inverse of that of absorption and exhibits similar features.

4 Each main current of migration produces a compensating counter-current.

5   Migrants proceeding long distances generally go by preference to one of the great centres of commerce and industry.

6   The natives of towns are less migratory than those of rural parts of the country.

7   Females are more migratory than males (Ravenstein 1889 p 169).

After more than eighty years it is surprising how many of these 'laws' are still valid. In a study of migration in upland Wales, H. R. Jones (1965) was able to confirm the existence of a significant distance-decay, the absorption of migrants in a leap-frogging fashion, a predominant out-migration partially counterbalanced by an in-migration, and the attraction of those classed as long-distance migrants to the cities of the Midlands and south-east England. Taeuber and Taeuber (1964) found similar patterns in a study of migration between cities and suburbs in the United States. In other words, irrespective of the environment, the 'laws' of migration are still relevant to an understanding of the size and direction of migration.

Since Ravenstein's seminal work, a series of studies have attempted to modify some of his generalizations and to express them in more specific terms. Three will be mentioned here.

1   *Gravity Model*. According to Zipf (1946) the amount of migration from a place, or a point on a surface, does not decline with simple linear *distance* from a second place, because it is necessary to take into account the population of the two places involved. Population size is viewed as a surrogate for the opportunities available in the two places as well as the degree of interaction between the two, which, of course, affects the level of knowledge of those opportunities. In these terms the Gravity Model may be expressed by the equation:

$$M_{ij} = K . \frac{P_i P_j}{d_{ij}}$$

where M_{ij} = numbers of migrants between places i and j
   P_i = population of place i
   P_j = population of place j
   d_{ij} = distance between places i and j
   K   = calibrating constant

Of course different forms of function for the decline with distance yield different forms in the Gravity Model equation, but in all cases the derivation is the same (see Unit 3 for its derivation). Considerable empirical explanation of the observed variation in migration across a continuous surface. This has led to the introduction of the concept of intervening opportunity (see Units 3 and 6).

2   *Intervening Opportunity Model*. Stouffer (1940) has agreed that the shortcomings of the Gravity Model was due to its failure to take into account the *intervening opportunities* which might exist between any two places. According to Stouffer,

> There is no necessary relationship between mobility and distance . . . the number of persons going a given distance is directly proportional to the number of intervening opportunities. The relation between mobility and distance may be said to depend on an auxiliary relationship, which expresses the cumulated (intervening) opportunities as a function of distance (Stouffer 1940 p. 846).

In surface terms this may be broadly interpreted as a 'plain' of low opportunity interspersed with a number of 'hills' of greater opportunities. Figure 3 is an attempt to express this in cartographic form. In this instance the potential migrant at X, with its low level of opportunities, in his decision to migrate has to balance the shorter distance and medium level of opportunities of, say, Y with that of the greater distance and higher opportunities of, say, Z.

Figure 3

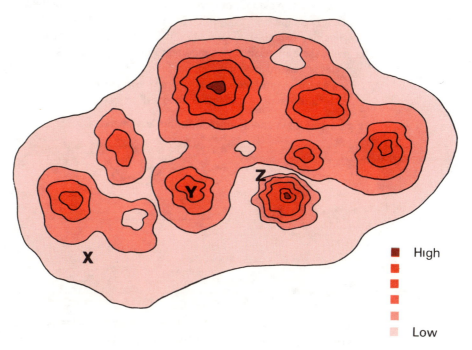

High

Low

This can be expressed by the formula:

$$M_{ij} = k \cdot \frac{P_i\,P_j}{IP_{ij}}$$

where IP_{ij} are the intervening opportunities between i and j

Underlying this concept is the premiss that migration is expensive and that the potential migrant will cease searching as soon as he finds an appropriate opportunity. The major handicap in testing this theory is that of defining 'opportunity'. In a study of migration in Cleveland, Stouffer (1940) used the number of vacant houses within a given census-defined area as an indicator of opportunities. Any vacancies existing as between two areas were regarded as 'intervening opportunities'. The analysis revealed considerable agreement between expected and observed values. In their study of net interstate migration in the United States in 1930, Bright and Thomas concluded that such migration

has in general followed the pattern of opportunities very closely . . . but . . . only if we allow for the major disturbances in the pattern attributable to qualitative differences in the opportunities sought in California and elsewhere and if allowance is made for the directional factor in the movement from the Middle West (Bright and Thomas 1941 p 783).

Isbell (1944) carried out a similar test of Stouffer's hypotheses on inter-county and intra-county migration in Sweden between 1921 and 1930, and again the results tended to substantiate the hypothesis. However, as a result of certain discrepancies between the expected and observed relationships between migration and intervening opportunities, Stouffer (1960) refined his theory by introducing an additional variable which he called 'competing migrants'. His revised model postulates that the total number of individuals migrating from place A to place B is a function of the number of opportunities at place B and an inverse function of the number of opportunities intervening between place A and place B, as well as of the number of other individuals competing for opportunities at place B. A recent study by Galle and Taeuber (1966) applied this new model to both the 1940 and 1960 census data of the United States. They found that the 1940 data fitted the model more closely than did the 1960 data, a fact which emphasizes the increasing complexity of the migration process.

3 Lee (1966) has argued that the distance and direction of migration is constrained by what he calls '*intervening obstacles*'. Such obstacles do not include only distance: . . . physical barriers like the Berlin Wall may be interposed, or immigration laws may

restrict the movement. Different people are, of course, affected in different ways by the same set of obstacles. What may be trivial to some people – the cost of transporting household goods, for example – may be prohibitive to others. The effect of a given set of obstacles depends also upon the impedimenta with which the migrant is encumbered. For some migrants these are relatively unimportant and the difficulty of surmounting the intervening obstacles is consequently minimal; but for others, making the same move, the impedimenta, among which we must reckon children and other dependants, greatly increase the difficulties posed by intervening obstacles (Lee 1966 p 48).

Figure 4 Origin and destination factors and intervening obstacles in migration

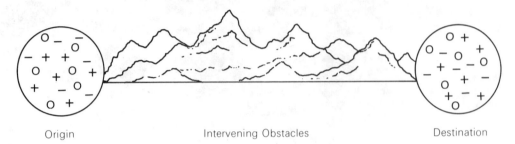

Origin   Intervening Obstacles   Destination

Source: Lee (1966)

Figure 4 is a representation of such intervening obstacles. At both the origin and the destination of migrants there are positive and negative factors (the zeros inside the circles indicate factors of no consequence, to which the potential migrant is indifferent); Lee sees the set of pluses and minuses as differently defined for every migrant or prospective migrant. The role of such obstacles in the migration process has long been recognized but has been expressed less directly. Except in terms of distance and intervening opportunities, these obstacles are extremely difficult to put to the test in any precise fashion.

Basically, all these recent postulations about the size and direction of migration are only refinements of Ravenstein's 'laws'. Essentially, these refinements present either a more precise testing of the 'laws' or a simplification of the migration process. However, both Ravenstein's 'laws' and their later modifications confirm that the size and direction of migration is guided by distance and intervening opportunities within the context of the individual's aspirations and his ability to overcome a series of intervening obstacles. Clearly, such forces will not operate uniformly for all potential migrants, and hence there is a tendency for a degree of migrant selectivity to exist. It is to the determination of such differential migration that we must now turn.

5.3 Who are the migrants?

Two of Ravenstein's seven 'laws of migration' indicated the existence of a certain degree of differential migration: that females are more migratory than males, and that the natives of towns are less migratory than those of rural parts of the country. Since the publication of Ravenstein's 'laws', a number of studies investigating the selective nature of migration have been carried out. By far the most significant has been the wide-ranging analysis undertaken by Dorothy S. Thomas in 1938. Using the evidence produced by Thomas and others, Beshers and Nishuira (1951) were able to postulate a series of generalizations concerning internal migration differentials. These generalizations are:

1 Young adults are the most mobile segment of the population.

2 Males tend to be more migratory than females.

3 Unemployed persons are more likely to move than employed persons.

4 Whites move more than non-whites.

5 Professionals are among the most mobile elements of the population.

However, a detailed review of the available empirical evidence on migration selectivity suggests that not all these hypotheses can be upheld in every situation. For example, in a study of migration among professional workers made on the basis of the United States 1960 census of population, Ladinsky (1967) concluded that age-differences were largely responsible for migration differentials, and that factors such as income, education, sex, family size, and marital status operated within the context of the life-cycle. In particular, he found that low income and high educational attainment operated to stimulate migration, whereas increased family size and advanced age dampened it. Surprisingly, Shryock (1958) concluded that non-whites in the United States had higher intra-county mobility rates than whites, although in total they had lower migration rates. A similar set of conclusions was reached by Andrei Rogers (1968) from his Markov-chain analysis of migration in California in 1960. Non-whites were more migratory than whites in urban to urban movements but lower in urban to suburban-rural moves: a clear indication of the obstacles to non-white suburban migration. The highest level of migration was recorded in the 15–19 and 20–24 age-groups and the lowest for the post-60 age-group. In contrast, from a study of migration in Chile, Herrick (1966) concluded that the characteristics of migrants were no different from those of non-migrants, except that migrant females were more frequently in the labour force than non-migrant ones. However, Zachariah (1962 and 1966) found in India that the number of male migrants exceeded that of female migrants, especially in long-distance and rural-urban streams, but that short-distance migration in rural areas was dominated by female migrants. More specifically, the migration flows to the cities, particularly Bombay, had high proportions of minority religious groups. Such case studies clearly emphasize the absence of a 'universal' set of migration differentials. In fact, it would appear that Bogue's comment on this point has considerable validity:

Only one migration differential seems to have systematically withstood the test – that for age. The following generalization has been found to be valid in many places and for long periods of time. Persons in their late teens, twenties and early thirties are much more mobile than younger or older persons. Migration is highly associated with the first commitment and acts of adjustment of adulthood that are made by adolescents as they mature (e.g. entrance into the labour force, marriage, family formation) (Bogue 1969).

However, this does not mean that migration selectivity does not take place. It would appear from the case studies quoted above that differential migration varies in character according to the nature of the environment and the population involved. This has led Bogue to put forward the notion that certain principles of selectivity can be identified under specified combinations of environmental and population conditions at places of origin and destination. These principles have been summarized by Jansen (1970) as follows:

1   There is a series of stages in the development of any major migration stream. From initial invasion it develops into a phase of settlement which at its peak becomes routine, institutionalized. In initial stages, men outnumber the women, but with the settlement phase sex selectivity tends to disappear or even favour women. During initial stages, migration is highly selective of young but mature adults, persons who are single, divorced or widowed.

2   Migration stimulated by economic growth, technological improvements, etc. attracts the better-educated. Conversely, areas tending to stagnation lose their better-educated and skilled persons first.

3   If between two population points streams of equal size tend to flow, neither making net gains, then the composition of migration streams in each direction tends to be of minimum selectivity. If the stream flowing in one direction is greater than that flowing in the other direction, there is a greater selectivity in both streams. But the place showing a net gain would have a greater proportion of males, young adults, single, divorced, and widowed, while the place having a net loss would have high proportions of 'migration failures' (returnees), employees of new establishments, local migrants 'passing through' on their way to bigger centres and retired migrants returning to their place of origin.

4   Where the 'push' factor is very strong (famine, drought, etc.) origin selectivity is at a minimum; where 'pull' stimulus is greater, there will be an appreciable selectivity.

5   In modern technological societies, major streams which flow between metropolitan centres tend to have very little selectivity of migrants (Jansen 1970 pp 15–16).

These hypotheses have once again emphasized the universality of age as a determinant of differential migration. It would appear that the operation of other factors in determining migration selectivity can therefore be interpreted only within the contest of this life-cycle dimension. Empirically, this can most clearly be seen from a recent study by Croze (1956) of rural-urban selectivity of migrants in France during the year 1952. For the purposes of the study, France was divided into five categories of region: (1) the Paris region; (2) large cities with populations over 50,000; (3) medium-sized cities with populations between 10,000 and 49,999; (4) small cities with populations below 10,000; and (5) rural areas. When the net migration levels of these areas are related to the ages of the migrants certain significant patterns begin to emerge. In the 21–29 age-group all the urban areas showed a net gain by migration: small cities 1,217, medium cities 1,008, large cities 2,252, and Paris 5,514; rural areas, on the other hand, experienced a net loss of 9,991. A similar pattern of migration was revealed by the 30–44 age-group: small cities gained 1,662, medium-sized cities 146, large cities 67 and Paris 1,465; rural areas lost 3,340. But in the 45–49 age-group the pattern of gains and losses begins to change: rural areas gained 9,272; on the other hand, small cities lost 1,404, large cities 3,289 and Paris 5,886. In the post-60 age-group rural areas gained 2,799, small cities 1,767 and medium-sized cities 722, while large cities and Paris lost, respectively, 1,527 and 3,761. Such figures reveal fairly conclusively that urban selectivity can be strongly influenced by age.

Despite the failure to identify universal differential migration variables apart from age, it may be concluded that individuals differently located in space and social structure have different degrees of knowledge about, and are able to benefit to differing extents from, opportunities available at places other than those in which they currently reside. The next section will therefore be concerned with how people decide to migrate in the light of such knowledge.

Figure 5   Generalized locational decision scheme

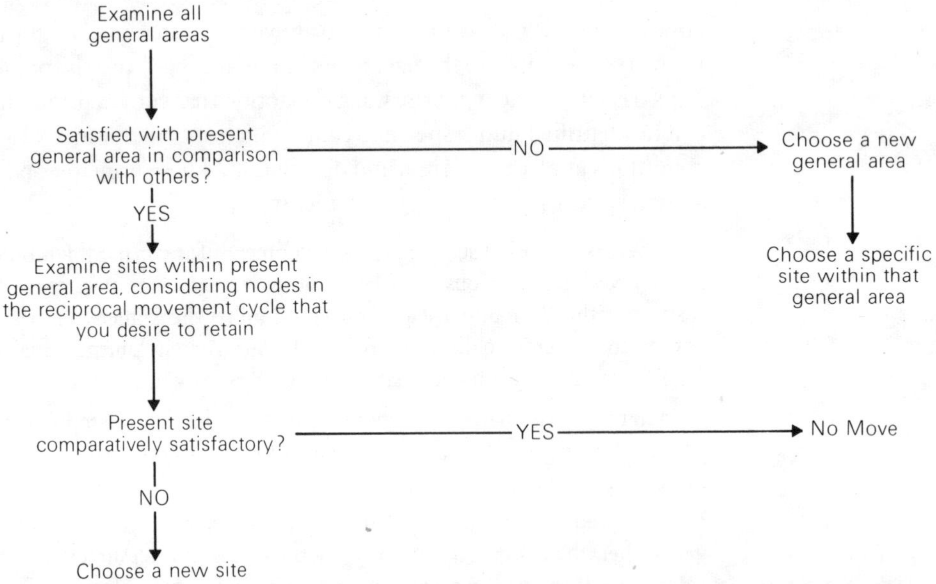

Source: Roseman (1971)

5.4   *How do people decide to migrate?*

Conceptually, the decision to migrate can be sub-divided into three stages: a first stage, in which a decision to seek a change of residence takes place; a second, in which an alternative location is selected; and a third, in which a decision whether or not to stay is made. The decision will in turn tend to consist of two successive steps (see Figure 5). In the first step a decision is made about the desired general *area* of residence. If a high evaluation is placed upon the present area and the current job, then migration beyond the commuting field of the place of work is unlikely. On the other hand, if a high evaluation is placed upon a better job or a better environment, in another area, then migration may take place. After this first decision has been made, another has to be made regarding the location of the *home* within the general area. This time the decision is based upon a comparative evaluation of the site and neighbourhood attributes of the present home with those of the potential alternative home. Migration does not take place if both the general-area and house-site decisions favour the present situation. Both decisions have to be made by all migrants. Of the two types of migrant, Total Displacement and Partial Displacement migrants, it is only the former who have to change their location as a result of both steps; the latter form of migration is based solely on the site and neighbourhood attributes of the home.

The comparative evaluation of the present location and potential future location is based upon the knowledge a migrant has concerning each alternative. The procedure by which an individual gathers such information is guided by the extent and content of his *information field*, or the set of places about which he has knowledge. Such a field can be divided into two: an *activity space* and an *indirect contact space* (Wolpert 1965). The former is made up of all those locations with which an individual has regular, almost day-to-day, contact. This contact results in a fairly accurate knowledge of the area involved, although it will be spatially rather restricted. Such knowledge forms the basis of the Partial Displacement migrant's decision. In contrast, indirect contact space lies beyond the area of the individual's day-to-day contacts, and here there is greater dependence upon the mass media and other people for information about alternative locations. The Total Displacement migrant's decision is more likely to be based upon this type of knowledge. The nature of such knowledge tends to make his site and neighbourhood decision less 'efficient' than that of the Partial Displacement migrant's, and so to increase the possibility that he himself will make a further Partial Displacement movement within a short interval of time.

It has long been established that within such an information-gathering process there tends to be a distance-decay as regards the accuracy and content of the information an individual possesses. However, within the indirect contact space of individuals, there also exists a series of biases, the principal ones being of a *connective* and *random* nature, which distort the distance decay of information. *Connective* biases in information sources are those which result from regular contact, irrespective of distance, with friends and relatives. Such contacts provide the potential migrant with considerable information about the home locations of friends and relatives, and this often becomes the basis for selecting a new place of residence. In addition, friends and relatives can assist migrants by contributing to a reduction in movement costs, and can aid the assimilation of the newcomer into a strange community. The effect of such information feedback is to create a distinctive migration stream between two places. *Random*, or chance, components are often of significance in explaining the origin of what appear at first sight to be anomalous patterns. An example of such a random factor was quoted in the *Sunday Times* in 1969 as means of explaining the high density of Indians in Southall, London:

... it developed out of a chance war-time contact. The personnel manager at Wolf's Rubber Factory had met members of a Sikh regiment in the Middle East. When the labour shortage in Southall became acute he knew where to turn. Immediately the areas became a focus for further Indian settlement as a result of information feedback by early settlers to friends and relatives (The *Sunday Times*, 13th July 1969).

The flow of information that a potential migrant receives varies with geographical scale. At the Partial Displacement level, the information flow is guided by the reciprocal movement cycle within a city; for example, such information tends to be sectoral, with its apex at the city centre, since it reflects the regular movement-patterns of individuals. At a regional, or even national, scale, distance-decay is of greater significance, though partly distorted by the location of friends and relatives. Superimposed upon such flow networks are the mass media, such as radio, television, newspapers, and magazines, which pass on information for the most part independently of the listener's or reader's location.

6 Patterns of migration

So far in this unit we have attempted to determine the components of the migration process within the context of a simple migration system. The purpose of this section is to illustrate the migration patterns that result from such processes, by means of two examples: Ghana and the United States. In this way some idea of the similarities and differences in the various patterns of migration will be conveyed.

6.1 Ghana

Despite the availability of a national census, the extent of migration in Ghana cannot be calculated directly from the returns, and it is necessary to resort to indirect methods. By far the most significant indicators of migration in Ghana are urban growth and labour-force movements. In 1960 the urban population of Ghana totalled over one-and-a-half million. Although the total population of the country trebled from 1921 to 1960 (6.7 million), the urban sector multiplied nine times. It has been calculated that at least forty per cent of this urban growth was due to migration and its natural increase, and close to thirty per cent to net migration alone (Caldwell 1961). In addition, it has been estimated that at least one-fifth of the migrants were foreign-born, and it would appear that annual migration across the Ghanaian frontier exceeds 300,000 people in each direction. Since 1948 the annual rate of migration has been increasing, and now stands at about five per cent of the total population per annum. An alternative indirect source for estimating the extent of migration is labour-force data. Berg has suggested, on the evidence of such data, that almost all those in paid agricultural employment and perhaps half of those in paid non-agricultural employment are temporary migrants. Overall, more than half of all those who work for remuneration are migrants.

Such widespread migration has both a distance and a directional bias (Caldwell 1968). In general, the majority of the migrations are over short distances. Even in the case of immigrants, two out of every three originate from adjoining countries. According to Caldwell two main streams of migration may be identified: movements from poorer to richer areas, and from rural to urban areas. Although the principal migration stream in 1960 was still directed to the cocoa farms and gold mines, the rural-to-urban movement was involving an increasing share of the population. Why and how such migrations take place in Ghana is rather difficult to determine, because there are no studies specifically concerned with these issues. Caldwell (1969) has argued that economic development in Ghana is focused on the towns, and that demands for labour in the majority of the urban areas cannot be met by the local supply. In addition, the growing industries of the southern areas of Ghana, with their need for labourers, have tended to attract migrants from the poorer and crowded northern areas. In other words, there is a simple 'push'-'pull' situation. Such migrations tend to take two forms: temporary movement, which is particularly characteristic of the immigrants, and a seasonal movement, which is favoured by the internal migrants. The seasonal migrants move in a circular fashion – from village to town and town to village. The growing significance of this net rural-to-urban migration, however, has led Caldwell to predict an increase in long-term internal migration, greater family movements, and a general decline in seasonal migration. A major component in determining the chosen destination of the permanent migrants is the location of friends and relatives. About 75 per cent of rural migrants indicated that they had received help from relatives and friends in finding a job, seeking accommodation, and obtaining money to make the journey from the village. It has been calculated that forty per cent stay at first with relatives and twenty-five per cent with friends.

Given that a large proportion of the migration is of a non-permanent type, and given the predominance of economic factors associated with migration, it is not surprising that young males formed the majority of the migrants. However, a recent survey indicates a reduction in the sex differentials of rural-to-urban migrants, thus further emphasizing the trend towards more permanent migration (Caldwell 1968). The propensity to migrate increases steadily with the size of the family: the rate ranges from thirty-three per cent among those with one or more male siblings to fifty per cent among those with five or more siblings. In addition, among the permanent migrants those who had received formal education were proportionately over-represented. Of those who migrated from rural to urban areas, less than a quarter had received no formal education, while two-thirds of those who had migrated had received secondary schooling. Clearly, this emphasizes the relationship between education and occupation, since without education a good job is highly unlikely. Both education and occupation are related to income and wealth. Indeed, taken together, these factors suggest the importance of the economic motive in Ghanaian migration, and the way in which the migration is tied to wealth and education.

6.2 The United States

Unlike Ghana, the United States has more detailed data available on contemporary migration. The 1960 national census contained a question about people's place of residence five years earlier, on April 1st 1955. From such a source Bogue (1969) has calculated that 50.1 per cent of the population (79.7 million) changed their place of residence during the period 1955–60. In fact, the actual number of moves was even greater, because a number of people moved several times.

According to Bogue the migration was largely localized in nature. He estimates that two-thirds of all migrants changed their residence within the same county. However, one migrant in ten crossed a major regional boundary, and so the significance of long-distance migration should not be under-estimated. Regionally, the North-East and North-Central regions lost a substantial number of migrants, the South made a small net gain, and the West a huge gain.

Irrespective of the distances involved in the migration, all but a tiny fraction arrived at an urban or suburban destination. Of every hundred out-migrants, seventy went to urban areas, twenty-six to rural non-farm areas, and four to farm residences. However, the proportional gain in population from migration was higher among the rural non-farm population than the urban ones, indicating the importance of the process of suburbanization.

Despite such widespread migration there was still a certain degree of selectivity of the population (Bogue 1969). Males appeared to be slightly, though only slightly, more migratory than females and were more inclined to migrate over long distances. Further, the median age of mobile persons was 22.9, though the age-pattern of migrants was similar for the two sexes. In the 25–45 age-group males were more mobile than females, although at the oldest ages this pattern tended to be reversed. The non-white population was considerably more migratory than the white population, and made overwhelmingly short-distance moves. No doubt this is a reflection of the struggle of non-whites to find adequate housing within the cities. Surprisingly, a higher proportion of the married than of the single population was found to be composed of migrants: the migrant has traditionally been pictured as an individual leaving the rural area to seek his fortune in the big city. Bogue suggests that there may be two explanations as to why this is not the case at present. Families now migrate as entities because corporations increasingly move workers from one place to another, and there is also a tendency for migrants to marry at an earlier age than resident non-migrants.

6.3 Discussion

Although the specific migration patterns identified in Ghana and the United States appear unique on their own, yet, when they are compared with each other, and even with other parts of the world, several parallels emerge:

1 Ghanaian migration is characterized by its temporariness and by concomitant high rates of return movements. A closely-related feature is that of seasonal migration. In the United States migration appears to be of a more permanent nature. However, the trend in Ghana is towards longer-term permanent migration.

2 The general extent of urbanization is low in Ghana as compared with the United States. But the patterns point to a more rapid increase, as migratory flows accelerate and as industrialization proceeds. Although the pace is different, the pattern is similar.

3 The importance of the economic motive in the migration process has been established in both Ghana and the United States.

4 In the case of Ghana chain migration is particularly significant.

The existence of such parallels and differences indicates the presence of considerable order in the migration process.

6.4 Conclusion

In this unit migration has been conceived in terms of a simple system. Change in one part of the system has a direct or indirect effect upon all other parts. Within such a system migration is a response to social, political, economic and cultural changes. Despite differential responses to such changes, there is considerable order in the ways in which individuals decide to migrate and in which their decisions are constrained by a variety of obstacles. The resultant patterns of migration, as revealed by studies of Ghana and the United States, exhibit considerable uniformity despite marked differences in these countries' economic and social structures.

Although for analytical purposes migration has been viewed as a dependent variable in this unit, it is quite clear that migration must also be viewed as an independent variable affecting change processes. In other words, the question arises: given a pattern of population movement, what social, political, economic and cultural consequences ensue? This will be the theme of Unit 10.

Self-assessment questions

SAQ 1   How would you define (a) migration (b) in-migration (c) out-migration (d) gross-migration?

SAQ 2   How would you differentiate between international and internal migration?

SAQ 3   What is the significance of the distinction between Reciprocal Movements and Migratory Movements for migration study?

SAQ 4   What are the weaknesses of census-based migration data?

SAQ 5   What is a migration system?

SAQ 6   What form does the *energy* within a rural–urban migration system take?

SAQ 7   Outline the 'push-pull' concept in determining migration.

SAQ 8   What is the Lowry model?

SAQ 9   Which of Beshers' and Nishuira's generalizations concerning migration differentials are upheld by empirical evidence?

SAQ 10   Identify the role of an individual's information field in the decision to migrate.

SAQ 11   Differentiate between an activity space and an indirect contact space.

SAQ 1   (a) *Migration* is the physical transition of an individual from one place or region to another; (b) *In-migration* is the entry of an individual into a place or region; (c) *Out-migration* is the departure of an individual from a place or region; (d) *Gross-migration* is the total number of individuals entering and leaving a place or region.

SAQ 2   International migration is the movement of people between nations, and internal migration the movement of people within a nation.

SAQ 3   Three factors may be suggested. First, the distinction emphasizes that migration is a part of the wider concept of human movement; second, that all human movements involve the home location; and third, the distinction between Total and Partial Displacement migratory movement is broadly analogous to that between inter-regional and inter-urban (or rural) migration respectively.

SAQ 4   Three may be suggested. First, there is the void created by the time-interval between successive censuses; second, details are available only for large areal units; third, nothing is said about why individuals migrate.

SAQ 5   A systems approach to migration views the process as a complex of interacting elements, together with their attributes and relationships. Migration is, therefore, conceived as a circular, inter-dependent and self-modifying system in which the effects of changes in one part have a ripple effect throughout the whole system.

SAQ 6   The *energy*, or driving force, within a rural-urban migration system can be equated with the stimuli to move acting on the rural individual. The stimulus to migrate can be related to the degree of integration of the rural economy to the national economy, to the degree of awareness of opportunities outside the rural areas, and to the social and economic expectations held by the rural population.

SAQ 7   The reasons why individuals migrate can be explained in terms of the relative attractions of different locations, or differential place-utilities. Within such a concept there is a series of forces which encourage an individual to leave one place (*push*) and attract him to another (*pull*). Such forces can be created, on the one hand, by changes within the environment, and, on the other, by changes in the personal motives of the individual.

SAQ 8   Briefly, the Lowry model predicts that the number of migrants between two regions can be explained in terms of differential economic opportunities. Within the original model such opportunities were identified by means of such indices as the number of persons in non-agricultural employment, unemployment as a percentage of the number in non-agricultural employment, hourly manufacturing wage, and the straight-line distance separating the two regions.

SAQ 9   Only one migration differential seems to have systematically withstood the test – that for age. However, this does not mean that migration selectivity does not take place. It would appear from the case studies quoted in 5.3 that differential migration varies in character according to the nature of the environment and the population involved.

SAQ 10 The decision to migrate is based upon a comparative evaluation of the present location and the potential future location. The procedure by which an individual gathers information about each alternative location is guided by the extent and content of his information field, or set of places about which he has knowledge.

SAQ 11 An activity space is made up of all those locations with which an individual has regular, almost day-to-day, contact. In contrast, indirect contact space lies beyond the area of the individual's day-to-day contacts, and here there is greater dependence upon the mass media and other people for information about alternative locations.

References BERG, E. (1965) 'The Economics of the Migrant Labour System', in H. Kuper (ed), *Urbanization and Migration in West Africa*, Los Angeles, University of California Press.

BESHERS, J. M. and NISHUIRA, E. N. (1961) 'A Theory of Internal Migration Differentials', *Social Forces*, 39, pp 214–18.

BOGUE, D. J. (1959) 'Internal Migration', in Hauser, P. M. and Duncan, O. D. (eds) (1959) *The Study of Population*, Chicago, University of Chicago Press.

BOGUE, D. J. (1961) 'Techniques and Hypotheses for the Study of Differential Migration', *International Population Conference*, paper 114.

BOGUE, D. J. (1969) *The Principles of Demography*, London, John Wiley.

BRIGHT, M. L. and THOMAS, D. S. (1941) 'Interstate Migration and Intervening Opportunities', *American Sociological Review*, 6, pp 773–83.

CALDWELL, J. C. (1961) 'Migration and Urbanization', in Birmingham, W. *et al*, *A Study of Contemporary Ghana*, Vol 2, London, George Allen and Unwin.

CALDWELL, J. C. (1968) 'Determinants of Rural-Urban Migration in Ghana', *Population Studies*, 22, pp 361–75.

CALDWELL, J. C. (1969) *African Rural-Urban Migration*, Canberra, Australian National University Press.

CAVALLI-SFORZA, H. (1962) 'The Distribution of Migration Distances: Models and Applications to Genetics', in Sutter, J. (ed) *Human Displacements*, Monaco.

CROZE, M. (1956) 'An Instrument for Studying Internal Migrations: Movements of Voters', *Population*, 2, pp 235–60.

DAVIES, W. K. D. (1966) 'Latent Migration Potential and Space Preferences', *Professional Geographer*, XVIII, pp 300–4.

EISENSTADT, S. (1954) *The Absorption of Immigrants : A Comparative Study Based on the Jewish Community in Palestine and the State of Israel*, London, Routledge and Kegan Paul.

GALLE, O. R. and TAEUBER, K. E. (1966) 'Metropolitan Migration and Intervening Opportunities', *American Sociological Review*, 31, pp 5–13.

HARRIS, A. I. and CLAUSEN, R. (1966) *Labour Mobility in Great Britain 1953–63*, London, Government Social Survey.

HERBERLE, R. (1938) 'The Causes of Rural-Urban Migration: A Survey of German Theories', *American Journal of Sociology*, 43, pp 932–50.

HERRICK, B. (1966) *Urban Migration and Economic Development in Chile*, MIT Monographs in Economics, 6, Cambridge, Mass., MIT Press.

ISBELL, E. C. (1944) 'Internal Migration in Sweden and Intervening Opportunities', *American Sociological Review*, 9, pp 627–39.

JANSEN, C. J. (ed) (1970) *Readings in the Sociology of Migration*, Oxford, Pergamon.

JONES, H. R. (1965) 'A Study of Rural Migration in Central Wales', *Transactions of the Institute of British Geographers*, 37, pp 31–45.

LADINSKY, J. (1967) 'Sources of Geographic Mobility among Professional Workers: A Multivariate Analysis', *Demography*, 4, pp 293–309.

LEE, E. S. (1966), 'A Theory of Migration', *Demography*, 3, pp 47–57.

LEWIS, G. J. (1969) *Socio-geographic Change in the Welsh Borderland since 1861*, University of Leicester unpublished PhD thesis.

LOWRY, I. S. (1966) *Migration and Metropolitan Growth: Two Analytical Models*, San Francisco, Chandler.

MABOGUNJE, A. K. (1970) 'Systems Approach to a Theory of Rural-Urban Migration', *Geographical Analysis*, 2, pp 1–18.

MANGALAM, J. J. (1968) *Human Migration*, Lexington, Ky., University of Kentucky Press.

OLIVER, F. (1964) 'Inter-regional Migration and Unemployment 1951–61', *Journal of the Royal Statistical Society*', 127, pp 42–75.

PETERSON, W. (1958) 'A General Typology of Migration', in C. J. Jansen (ed) *Readings in the Sociology of Migration*, Oxford, Pergamon.

POURCHER, G. (1963) *Le peuplement de Paris* (The Peopling of Paris), *Population*, 3, pp 545–64.

RAVENSTEIN, E. G. (1889) 'The Laws of Migration', *Journal of the Royal Statistical Society*, 48, pp 167–235.

RODGERS, A. (1970) 'Migration and Industrial Development: The Southern Italian Experience', *Economic Geography*, 46, pp 111–35.

ROGERS, A. (1968) *Matrix Analysis of Interregional Population Growth and Distribution*, Berkeley, University of California Press.

ROSEMAN, C. C. (1971) 'Migration as a Spatial and Temporal Process', *Annals of the Association of American Geographers*, 61, pp 589–98.

ROSSI, P. H. (1965) *Why Families Move: A Study in the Social Psychology of Urban Residential Mobility*, Glencoe, Ill., Free Press.

SHRYOCK, H. S. (1958) 'The Efficiency of Internal Migration in the United States', *International Union for the Scientific Study of Population*, Vienna, pp 685–94.

SJASTAAD, L. A. (1962) 'The Cost and Returns of Human Migration', *Journal of Political Economy*, 70, pp 80–95.

STOUFFER, S. (1940) 'Intervening Opportunities: a Theory Relating Mobility and Distance', *American Sociological Review*, 5, pp 846–67.

STOUFFER, S. (1960) 'Intervening Opportunities and Competing Migrants', *Journal of Regional Science*, 2, pp 1–26.

SUNDAY TIMES, The, 13th July 1969, p 15.

TAEUBER, K. and TAEUBER, A. (1964) 'White Migration and Socio-economic Differences between Cities and Suburbs', *American Sociological Review*, 29, pp 718–29.

THOMAS, B. (1959) 'International Migration' in Hauser, P. M. and Duncan, O. D. (eds) (1959) *The Study of Population*, Chicago, University of Chicago Press, pp 510–43.

THOMAS, D. S. (1938) *Research Memorandum on Migration Differentials*, Social Science Research Council Bulletin 43, New York.

WOLPERT, J. (1965) 'Behavioural Aspects of the Decision to Migrate', *Papers and Proceedings, Regional Science Association*, 15, pp 159–69.

ZACHARIAH, K. C. (1962) *Historical Study of Internal Migration in the Indian Sub-Continent 1901–31*, Bombay, Demographic Training and Research Centres.

ZACHARIAH, K. C. (1964) *Population Redistribution in India*, Bombay, Research Report to UN Demographic Research and Training Centre.

ZACHARIAH, K. C. (1966) 'Bombay Migration Study: A Pilot Analysis of Migration in an Asian Metropolis', *Demography*, 37, pp 378–92.

ZIPF, G. K. (1946) 'The $P_1 P_2/D$ Hypothesis in the Intercity Movement of Persons', *American Sociological Review*, 11, pp 677–86.

Acknowledgements Grateful acknowledgement is made to the following sources for material used in this unit:

Figures

Figures 1 and 5: reproduced by permission from the *Annals* of the Association of American Geographers, 61, 1971: *Figure 2:* reprinted from 'Systems approach to a theory of rural–urban migration' by Akin L. Mabogunje in *Geographical Analysis*, 2, January 1970, copyright © 1970 by the Ohio State University Press. All rights reserved: *Figure 4:* Population Association of America for E.S. Lee, 'A theory of migration' in *Demography*, 3, 48, 1966.

Tables

Table 1: The American Sociological Association and the author for W. Peterson, 'A general typology of migration' in *American Sociological Review*, 23, 3, 1958.

Unit 10
The consequences of labour migration

Prepared by Gareth Lewis

Contents

		Page
1	Introduction	35
2	Societal consequences of migration	35
2.1	Migration in Ghana	35
2.2	Redistribution of population	36
2.3	Redistribution of social groups	38
2.4	Changing distribution of the labour force	39
2.5	Socio-political problems	41
3	Community consequences of migration	41
3.1	Differential population growth	41
3.2	Urban growth	43
3.3	Rural decline	44
3.4	Rural growth	45
4	Individual consequences of migration	46
4.1	Nature of assimilation	46
4.2	Acculturation	47
4.3	Adjustment	48
4.4	Participation	49
4.5	Stages of assimilation	49
5	Conclusion	50
	Self-assessment Questions	50
	References	52

1	Introduction	Although the preceding unit was concerned with the nature of migration as a response to social, political, economic and cultural changes within society, it is quite clear that migration can also be viewed as an independent variable, since it can initiate change itself. In other words, given a pattern of labour mobility, what social, political, economic and cultural consequences ensue? However, it should be borne in mind that migration is only one of many agents which can initiate change. Among others which are of considerable significance are the dissemination of new ideas, information and techniques by means of spatial diffusion (Rogers 1962, Hägerstrand 1967).

It is generally assumed that labour migration has a beneficial effect on regional development. Such an assessment is based upon economic criteria, and, despite considerable research, the non-economic consequences of migration have too often been overlooked. This is rather surprising, when it is recalled that the greater part of this research has emphasized that migrants tend to experience considerable problems of adjustment and conflict as well as personal and community disorganization. Clearly, before a meaningful assessment can be made of the benefits of labour mobility its social, political, and cultural consequences need to be discussed. Such a topic therefore necessitates a detailed examination in its own right.

Basically there are two major questions involved in any study of the consequences of migration:

1 What are the effects of migration upon the area of origin and the area of destination?

2 What effects does the process of migrating have on individuals who undergo it?

Since these effects can take place at several scales of society, notably the whole society, the community, and the individual, this three-way distinction of societal scales will form the basis of the major division of this unit. In addition, empirical evidence will provide the background to the generalizations presented here, because no sound theoretical base exists on which we can analyse the impact of labour migration (Matras 1973).

2	Societal consequences of migration	The societal consequences of migration involve changes in the socio–economic structure of society. Migration not only acts as the mechanism by which the socio–economic surface undergoes change but also initiates further change itself. Such changes are diffuse and complex, since they involve, either directly or indirectly, all parts of the surface. In order that the principal societal consequences may be identified, this section will begin with a brief analysis of the implications of migration within a particular nation-state: Ghana has again been chosen as an example. After the major societal consequences of migration within Ghana have been outlined, the nature of each of them will then be discussed within the context of a series of surfaces.

2.1	*Migration in Ghana*	According to Caldwell (1961 p 139) '. . . migration has profoundly affected Ghana, and its effect is a reflection of the depth of the economic and social changes which have occurred this century. It, in its turn, is an agent of further change.' A primary demographic consequence of migration has been to redistribute the population, particularly in the direction of the urban areas. In Unit 9 it was shown that about two-thirds of urban growth in Ghana during recent decades is a function of internal and external migration. Moreover, it is becoming apparent that the younger and more skilled members of the society are more concentrated in towns than in rural village areas. However, Caldwell (1968) has argued that the high rates of natural increase in rural areas and high rates of return migration reduce the equilibrium function of migration. In other words, the reduction in the excess rural population through mobility to urban areas has been less than dramatic.

Many scholars view the migrant labour system in Ghana and other West African States as an efficient adaptation to a changing economy. Migration has permitted such countries to experience more rapid economic growth than might otherwise have been possible. Berg (1965) has gone as far as to argue that labour migration has been an economic benefit to the labour-exporting villages and not only to recipient areas. Nevertheless, others claim that temporary migration makes labour productivity lower than it would be if the same labour force were permanent: temporary migration prevents the establishment of a permanent industrial labour force, discourages the acquisition of skills and the development of labour organization, and may lead to social problems in recipient areas where migrants of different origins are brought together. Further, it can also be argued that seasonal migration is detrimental to the labour-exporting rural communities. Skinner (1966) has shown that among the Mossi of the Upper Volta region migration has affected agricultural practices, the types of crops grown, and work patterns. Seasonal migration has resulted in the discontinuance of family farming, since every hand available was required to make it operative. In addition, attitudes towards farming have changed, from the pursuit of subsistence to commercial ideals. As a result, many of the Mossi have given up agriculture in order to engage in local and regional trading. Although labour migration has changed the economic and material life of the Mossi, it is far from clear whether it has resulted in any substantial improvement in their standard of living.

On the other hand, migration strengthens the economic infrastructure through the need to develop roads and transportation facilities. As a result of migration between rural and urban areas in Ghana, the cash economy is beginning to spread to the rural districts, and Goldschreider (1971) has gone so far as to claim that migration may prove instrumental in stimulating industrialization in the larger towns: 'Rather than serving as a response to rapid industrialization and the need for an urban labour supply, migration in Africa may stimulate industrialization and generate economic development' (Goldschreider 1971 p 210).

However, despite the apparent economic advantages of labour migration, seasonal movements can cause considerable social and political problems. This temporary migration means the disruption of agricultural production and authority structure in rural areas. In the towns, it means the establishment of a permanent unskilled labour force, and a young, male, potentially violent population. For society as a whole it may mean unemployment and group tensions. One such tension associated with migration is the discord it engenders in authority, family, and kinship relationships.

The discussion of Ghana has revealed the existence of four major societal consequences of migration: a redistribution of population, a change in the distribution of given types of people, a change in the distribution of the size and structure of the labour force, and the development of certain social and political difficulties within the society. Having identified such consequences of migration in a non-spatial context, let us in the remainder of this section analyse their nature and significance for the changing gradients of different types of surfaces.

2.2 Redistribution of population

The migratory movement of individuals is, by definition, a mechanism by which the spatial distribution of population is altered or transformed. However, the measurement of such population transformations is complicated by two factors. Firstly, migration can be viewed either from the point of origin of the population or from its point of destination; secondly, migration between any two parts of a surface can involve movement in both directions, so that it may be necessary to differentiate between net and gross migration. A number of techniques have been evolved to measure the degree of population redistribution. However, in any such measurement it is necessary to apply the outflow rates to each of the original populations and combine the numbers of migrants to each of the destinations. This can be represented in a matrix-like form in the following manner:

$$\left\{ \begin{array}{l} \text{End–of–interval} \\ \text{population in first} \\ \text{category} \end{array} \right\} = \left\{ \begin{array}{l} \text{Beginning–of–interval} \\ \text{population in first} \\ \text{category} \end{array} \right\} \times \left\{ \begin{array}{l} \text{First category to} \\ \text{first category} \\ \text{outflow rate} \end{array} \right\}$$

36

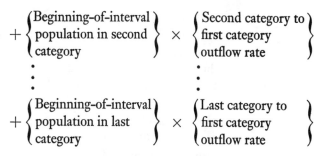

$$+ \left\{\begin{array}{l}\text{Beginning-of-interval}\\ \text{population in second}\\ \text{category}\end{array}\right\} \times \left\{\begin{array}{l}\text{Second category to}\\ \text{first category}\\ \text{outflow rate}\end{array}\right\}$$

$$\vdots \qquad\qquad \vdots$$

$$+ \left\{\begin{array}{l}\text{Beginning-of-interval}\\ \text{population in last}\\ \text{category}\end{array}\right\} \times \left\{\begin{array}{l}\text{Last category to}\\ \text{first category}\\ \text{outflow rate}\end{array}\right\}$$

Thus, the rates in the outflow operate to alter the population from its initial distribution at the beginning of the interval to its subsequent distribution at the end. The procedure can be represented as:

$$\Pi_0\, M_1 = \Pi_1$$

where Π_0 is the initial population, M_1 is the outflow-table matrix, and Π_1 is the subsequent population.

More generally, populations are subject to sequences of migration regimes $M_1, M_2, M_3 \ldots M_k$, in the first, second, third, ... k-th intervals, which continuously effect shifts in the distribution of population, resulting in $\Pi_1, \Pi_2, \Pi_3 \ldots \Pi_k$ etc. (Barclay 1958, A. Rogers 1968, Pressat 1972).

By means of such measurement techniques, certain changes in the gradient of a demographic surface may be identified. Gibbs (1963), for example, has argued that the redistribution of population in industrialized societies during the past two hundred years or so has been characterized by considerable spatial order. He maintains that urbanization involves, not only an increase in the size of towns and cities, but also a tendency towards concentrations of population in certain parts of the demographic surface. According to Gibbs such population redistribution takes place in a series of distinct stages.

1   Cities come into being, but the percentage increase of the rural population equals or exceeds that of the urban population at the time that cities first appear.
2   The percentage increase of the urban population comes to exceed the percentage increase of the rural population.
3   The rural population undergoes an absolute decline.
4   The population of small cities undergoes an absolute decline.
5   The difference among the territorial divisions with regard to population density declines, i.e. a more even spatial distribution of population develops.

Of course such stages are not mutually exclusive; consequently, it is logically possible for a society to be at two or more of the stages simultaneously. Gibbs attempted to identify these stages in the redistribution of population in the United States during the past 100 years or so. Broadly, he found that they were an adequate description of the redistribution of population in the United States. Shryock's study (1964) supports this conclusion:

... The current trend of geographic redistribution involves movement out of the heartland of the United States to the seacoasts and to the shores of the Great Lakes. There has apparently been a net migratory movement from rural to urban areas for a long time. Within metropolitan areas there is now a centrifugal movement of population; most large cities are losing people in the interchange with their own suburbs (Shryock 1964 pp 63–4).

A number of other studies have lent considerable support to Gibbs's theory of population concentration: studies of Hungary, for example, (Compton 1969), the United States (Rogers 1969), and Britain (Osborne 1955). However, population transformations are not the only societal effects of migration. All migrations tend to be selective – that is, they include certain types of people and exclude others – so that, far from there being a simple redistribution of the total population, there is a changing distribution of given types of people in distinct ways.

Unfortunately, studies of the redistribution of social groups in surface terms are extremely limited. Although theory maintains that such changes would be expected in most societies, the absence of sufficient data makes it extremely difficult to verify this empirically. However, a number of recent studies in England and Wales have gone some way towards filling this void. Hall and Smith (1968), Coates and Rawstron (1966), and Waugh (1969) have identified considerable variation in the distribution of status groups in England and Wales. Waugh, in particular, was concerned with the changing distribution of status groups. By taking occupations of a management and professional nature (Socio-Economic Groups 1, 2, 3 and 4) as indicators of high status, Waugh attempted to explain changes in the pattern of high-status groups in response to differential migration rates. As Figure 1 shows, the

Figure 1   Distribution of high-status groups in 1961

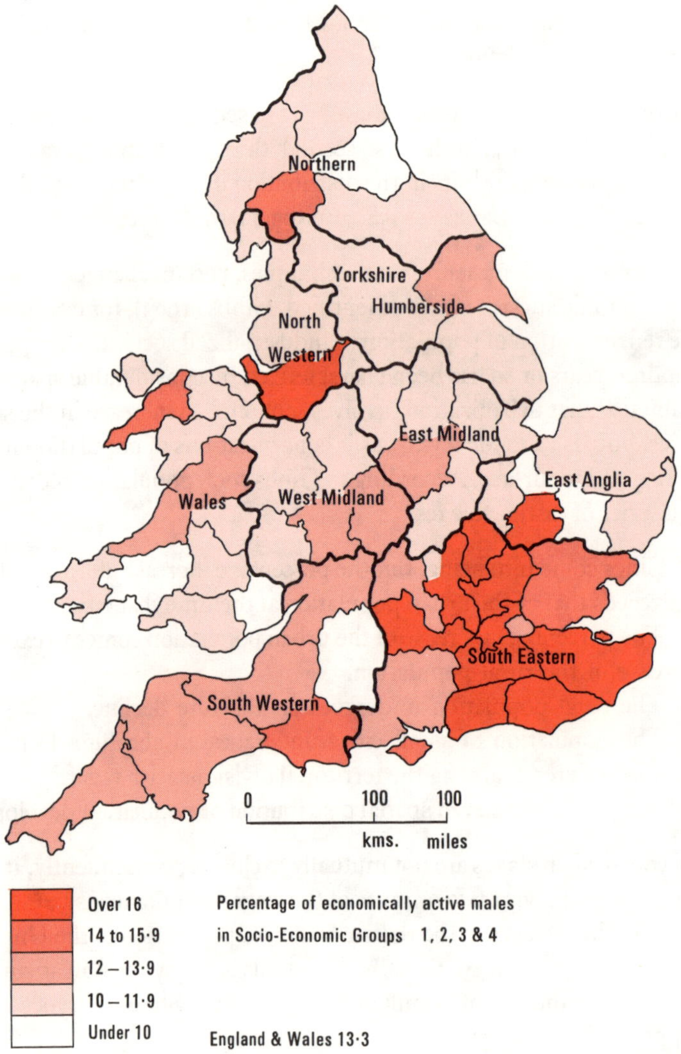

Percentage of economically active males
in Socio-Economic Groups   1, 2, 3 & 4

Over 16
14 to 15·9
12 — 13·9
10 — 11·9
Under 10

England & Wales 13·3

Source: Waugh (1969)

largest concentration of high-status groups was in the counties in and around London, and to a lesser extent on the west and south coast. Those counties with a dearth of professional and managerial workers included both agricultural and heavy-industry areas. Such a surface is characterised by a simple gradient stretching from the 'high' of the south-east to the 'low' of the north, east and Wales, which is occasionally punctuated with isolated 'highs'. By 1966 (Figure 2) the counties of the South Midlands, East Anglia, the South-West, and around London had gained high-status migrants, whilst a number of counties in the West Midlands, Wales and the North had experienced a loss. Although it is fairly clear that those counties with a higher proportion of professional and managerial residents in 1961 were the areas of greatest attraction for high-status people during the next five years, a certain number of

38

Figure 2 Gains and losses among economically active male residents in high-status groups through inter-regional migration, 1961-6

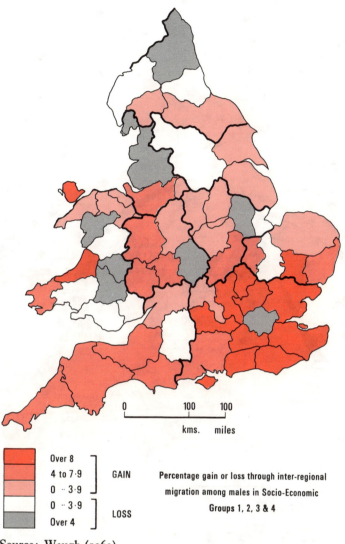

Over 8
4 to 7·9   } GAIN
0 - 3·9

0 - 3·9   } LOSS
Over 4

Percentage gain or loss through inter-regional migration among males in Socio-Economic Groups 1, 2, 3 & 4

Source: Waugh (1969)

additional foci were beginning to develop: for example, there were gains in high-status migrants by the North Riding of Yorkshire, peripheral counties of the Midlands, parts of the North region, and Wales. According to Waugh such changes were due to structural changes in particular regions' economies. The expansion of high-status employment not only creates opportunities for social mobility for the resident population but also provides a focus for migrants from outside. In addition, the increasing divorce of place of work from place of residence contributes significantly to the changing location of the high-status groups. However, in broad terms, this involves the accentuation of the contrast between the South-east and the remainder of England and Wales.

2.4 *Changing distribution of the labour force*   Such changes in the demographic surface, both in terms of density and social groups, does not always fulfil the needs of industry and commerce. Therefore, in certain countries there is a need to attract a pool of temporary workers to carry out specific tasks. In Ghana and other African States seasonal migration is an established part of the migration system, but, surprisingly, it is also still a significant factor in the economic organization of many industrial countries. Recently the United Nations estimated that there are as many as eight million temporary migrants in Europe, and that another eleven million will be needed by 1985. The sources of such migrants include Greece, Spain, Portugal, Turkey, Yugoslavia, and North Africa (Figure 3).

Figure 3   Migrant workers in the EEC

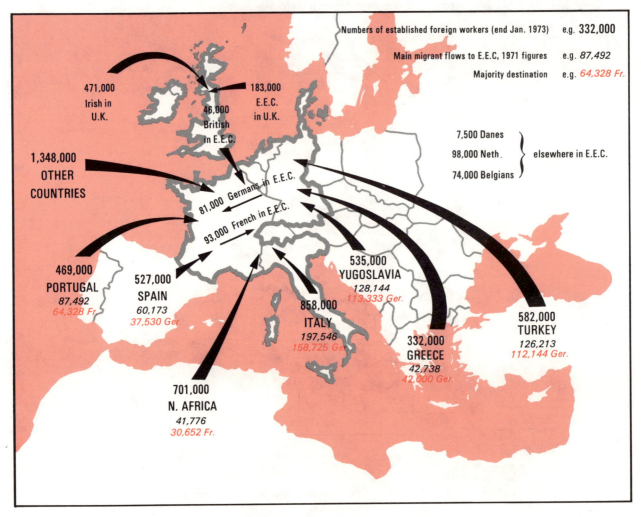

Source: *Sunday Times*, July 22nd 1973

An article in the Sunday Times (1973) has claimed that one in every ten workers from these countries earns his living in Europe. The majority of these migrants are involved in unskilled tasks.

Temporary migration of this kind contains the seeds of future economic problems, particularly for the native lands of the migrants. In the case of the European immigrants the Sunday Times estimates that they earn nearly £2,000 million. Although the £1,000 million that the migrants send home is a vital contribution to the economies of their native countries, the additional £1,000 million left on deposit in Europe could be vital capital for further economic development. For other reasons, too, a number of countries are already beginning to question the value of letting so many of their best workers (for example, thirty per cent of Yugoslavia's emigrants are skilled) leave for Western Europe. In Turkey there is a shortage of skilled foremen and supervisors and small entrepreneurs, whilst in Athens building labour is so difficult to find that Egyptians are being brought in to replace the locals who have left for West Germany and elsewhere. Such a migration pattern is analogous to a series of 'waves' directed towards the major centres of commerce and industry. However, even for the countries of Western Europe an over-dependence on such labour may prove to be a short-sighted policy, since stricter emigration policies in the native countries of the temporary migrants may easily induce economic difficulties.

2.5 Socio-political problems

Any differential migration which involves the whole society cannot take place without effecting some kind of socio-political reaction in various parts of the demographic surface. In the areas experiencing an influx of migrants the nature of the socio-political problems once again can be illustrated by the case of the temporary migrant workers in Western Europe. According to the Sunday Times (1973), anti-immigration tension in European society and the new-found voice of the migrants themselves are possibly leading to a crisis. There is a need for more migrants, and those already in European countries are demanding a better way of life. They are increasingly prepared to fight as a group for opportunities to rise above the lowest jobs. But the more the migrants struggle to better themselves, the more they are seen as a threat by the natives. The ability of the migrant workers to act as a group is illustrated by the case of the protest strike by Africans in France in 1973:

Nearly 30,000 North African workers began a 24-hour strike in and around Marseilles . . . in protest at the recent wave of anti-Arab violence, in which seven Algerians have died. The violence followed the murder of a Marseilles bus driver by a deranged Algerian 10 days ago (*The Guardian* September 4th 1973).

In 1973, as a result of serious race riots in the Netherlands, Rotterdam put a ceiling on the number of migrants who can work there. Despite restrictions of this kind, there is a dawning realization in most of Western Europe that the migrants may be permanent, and so the call to 'send them home' is spreading rapidly among the lower-paid natives. Surprisingly even in those areas experiencing an efflux of migrants a similar type of socio-political reaction is taking place. In the case of the United Kingdom this is well illustrated by the growth of nationalism in Wales and Scotland. A number of political scientists have suggested that the recent advancement of such a movement is the result of a contraction in the amount of economic and social opportunities to be found in Scotland and Wales, which contrasts to their expansion in large parts of England. To the people that remain the resultant out-migration is seen as the agent which is destroying the fabric of native society.

3 Community consequences of migration

The community consequences of migration depend upon the intensity of the migration, its differential nature, and the social composition of the communities involved. It is now well established that, of the three components of population change (births, deaths, and migration), it is migration which is by far the most significant at the community level. Not only does migration bring about a net gain or loss of population, but by its selectivity, particularly of the young, it can also indirectly affect a community's population-growth rate. A continuous in-migration of young migrants can accelerate the birth-rate of the community involved; conversely, a large out-flow of young migrants contributes to a falling birth-rate. In the former case an accelerating natural increase will develop, whilst in the latter there will be a falling natural increase, or even a natural decrease. However, such migration affects the growth rates of different communities to different extents, as is shown below. In this instance communities may be regarded as a series of points on the demographic surface.

3.1 Differential population growth

As outlined in the previous unit, migration affects community population-growth rates in both contemporary Ghana and the United States. Broadly, it was shown that
(a) urban areas experienced a rapid population increase;
(b) the larger the urban areas, the greater the population increase;
(c) there was a fall in population in the rural areas;
(d) more specifically, in the case of the United States there was a growth in population in rural areas adjacent to urban areas.

In both countries this differential community population growth rate was overwhelmingly characterized by differences in the levels of migration as between various communities located across a surface.

Aldkogius (1970), in a study of population change and urban growth in Sweden, was able to identify a similar pattern. During the 1950s the population of urban places increased by 800,000 persons whilst that of rural areas declined by 350,000. The actual population increase was concentrated, however, in very restricted areas in the central and southern parts of the country: mainly in the larger urban centres. Urban places with more than 50,000 inhabitants are expected to increase their population by fifty per cent between 1950 and 1980, while the population of Sweden is expected to grow only twenty per cent during the same period. Smaller urban places, and not only the rural areas, have stagnated or declined in population.

However, during the 1960s in Europe further changes have taken place in the population-growth patterns of communities as a result of differential migration. Such tendencies may be illustrated by migration trends in England and Wales between 1961 and 1966 (Jansen 1969, Lind 1969). These trends may be broadly derived from Table 1 (see below). There were:

1 an outward migration from conurbations and major cities;
2 an inward migration to the smaller cities;
3 a rural increase in population.

Table 1
Population change in England and Wales, 1951–61, by type of area (residence).

Type of Area	Population		Total Change % per year	Change by migration % per year
	1951	1961		
Conurbations	16,923	16,900	−0.01	−0.46
Urban Areas of 100,000+	6,088	6,256	+0.27	−0.19
Urban Areas of 50–100,000	3,728	4,269	+1.36	+0.90
Urban Areas of less than 50,000	8,681	9,479	+0.88	+0.54
Rural districts	8,337	9,200	+0.99	+0.51

Source: Lind (1969)

Despite the continued increase in employment opportunities within the conurbations and major cities, the outward migration is a reflection of an increased divorce between place of work and residence. This is partly because rural areas and towns peripheral to the conurbations have become foci for in-migrants who work in the conurbations themselves. But there are also additional groups of out-migrants from the conurbations and major cities who have made moves beyond their orbit. Firstly, there are retired migrants who have located themselves in coastal districts or in the countryside; secondly, there are many single persons who were previously attracted to large cities, London in particular, but who upon marriage and fatherhood have found the economic and social stresses of raising a family so considerable that they have migrated out to the smaller cities. As a third case, Lind (1969) has argued that a typical 'inter-regional migrant seems very likely to be someone leaving one of the Northern conurbations and moving to a small town in the Midlands or South. This is very different from the normally accepted stereotype of migration which is of people leaving the uncongested north and moving to London' (Lind 1969 p 85).

These summaries of case studies have revealed the existence of three major community consequences of migration: urban growth, suburbanization, and rural decline. However, such consequences involve not only differential population growth but also considerable social change. The three consequences will be discussed in the remainder of this section.

3.2 Urban growth It has already been established that migration contributes significantly to the differential growth of towns and cities. At the same time it has been claimed that migration is the mechanism through which a city expands spatially. When the industrial cities were undergoing rapid growth through migration, the majority of the newcomers settled in the older inner areas of the city, which were vacated by the long-established residents in favour of the suburbs. After a period of adjustment and socialization, lasting one or more generations, the migrants would move to better housing areas on the periphery (Park, Burgess and McKenzie 1925). Such a pattern of growth and social change seems to have been the typical one for many European immigrants in North American cities, although, despite considerable social and geographical mobility, most American cities have retained a series of 'ethnic' neighbourhoods. For example, in *The Urban Villagers*, Gans (1962) described a distinctive Italian-American working-class neighbourhood in Boston, while Rees (1970) has drawn attention to a whole series of such neighbourhoods in contemporary Chicago. However, in recent years many scholars have begun to question the validity of this classical theory of migration and urban growth, on two major grounds:

1 The pattern of migration into the city envisaged by the theory does not correspond with the reality of the situation in cities experiencing high rates of in- and out-migration. Different groups of in-migrants move directly into different zones within the city: for example, the high-status migrants from other urban areas tend to locate themselves on the suburban fringes whilst young adults, both the unmarried and those married but without children, select the inner-city areas because they have certain economic and cultural advantages (Davies and Lewis, 1974).
2 Increasingly, evidence is being gathered which conclusively shows that not all migrants are able to achieve social and spatial mobility. A number of groups find it difficult, and in some cases almost impossible, to leave the inner city. According to Eisenstadt (1954) the development of this segregation is determined by changes in the role-allocation structure of both the migrant groups and the host society. In such a schema the formation on the one hand of groups with common cultural origins and of specialized religious, educational or other institutions serving migrants, and the existence on the other hand of community patterns of residential, occupational or social segregation, are both subsumed under the rubric of differences in roles allotted to, and performed by, migrants and non-migrants respectively. Community change may tend either towards *convergence* of role distribution (the *filtering* process) or towards the *stabilization* of separate, pluralistic role structures (the *segregation* process). Two major approaches have been developed to attempt to explain such segregation.

Rex and Moore (1967) view the migration of an individual as a class struggle for housing. Basing themselves on the British case, they argue that a population may be divided into several competing 'housing classes' with different positions in a market that is governed by extreme scarcity. In Britain the ability to obtain a mortgage or a council tenancy is crucial, and these are awarded according to entirely different criteria. A council tenancy depends upon proof of 'housing need', combined with long residence in the city, and this gives rise to a political conflict between established residents and newcomers, who are effectively precluded from council housing. This is the basis of Rex and Moore's argument as to why certain ethnic groups tend to remain within an inner city ghetto. Rex (1968) maintains that racial or ethnic prejudices that might arise from psychological or other sources are of little importance, and explicitly excludes racial discrimination. Rather, the discrimination experienced by the immigrant is interpreted as discrimination against him solely as a *newcomer* and a member of a particular housing class.

However, such an analysis fails to explain adequately why some migrants to the city eventually move from the inner city while others find themselves confined to a perpetual 'ghetto'. Increasingly, evidence seems to point towards *racial* prejudice and discrimination as the major factor preventing the geographical dispersion and social mobility of some migrant groups. Taeuber and Taeuber (1964), in a study of Chicago, tried to discover whether an 'urban Negro population can fruitfully be viewed as an immigrant population, comparable to European immigrant populations of earlier decades' (Taeuber and Taeuber 1964 p 374). Their comparative analysis revealed that Negroes exhibited a much greater tendency towards residential concentration than immigrant groups (including Puerto Ricans) who had a lower socio-economic status and who were linguistically less acculturated than the Negro population. Moreover, since sixty-five per cent of the Negro population had resided either in Chicago or a comparable city for over twenty years, their segregation could not be explained by lack of adaptation to urban conditions. In other words, the Negro population are subject to much greater discrimination than other minority groups in attempting to obtain mortgages, buy houses, and rent accommodation. Ward (1971), in a study of nineteenth-century North American cities, and Rose (1972), in a study of the contemporary city, have been able to confirm the findings of Taeuber and Taeuber.

3.3 Rural decline

The depopulation of rural areas within the developed world remains a paradoxical phenomenon, when one considers that the majority of developed nations are still experiencing considerable population growth. For example, in the United States an annual average of 2.8 million has been added to its population since 1950. Two-thirds of the United States population are concentrated in little more than 200 metropolitan centres, and about eighty-five per cent of all population growth is taking place in these areas. Although rural life has today become increasingly similar to urban life in many respects – for example, as regards material possessions, educational levels, and life-styles – the demographic situation of many rural areas has never been more divergent from that of the cities than it is now.

In a study of population change in the United States, Beale (1964) claimed that more counties had lost population during a period of high national population growth (the 1950s) than did so during the period of lowest national growth (the 1930s). In addition, it was shown that during the last four decades the proportion of losing counties that have been heavy losers has grown: in the 1920s little more than a fourth of the declining counties fell in population by more than ten per cent, but by the 1950s the proportion of losers in this class exceeded one-half. A similar pattern can be identified in England and Wales during the first half of the twentieth century (Osborne 1964). Surprisingly, some depopulation may also be identified in parts of the developing world. A recent study in Southern India has revealed the existence of a considerable rural depopulation in areas within the orbit of Madras (Arunchalam et al 1972). The predominant mechanism which brings about such depopulation is a net out-migration over a relatively lengthy period of time.

In the United States, as a result of a prolonged and increasingly high net out-migration of young rural adults (25–45 years old), a condition has been reached in many rural communities in which births are exceeded by the number of deaths taking place (Beale 1964). In such communities there exists a distorted age-structure, and an accelerating depopulation (Figure 4). In addition, the conceptions of traditional levels of rural-settlement density have to be altered. For example, parts of Missouri and Iowa, in the Corn Belt, today have only 15 persons per square mile, including urban areas, whereas at one time densities of less than 25 or 30 per square mile were unheard of. In Britain, a similar pattern has been revealed in detail for such rural areas as mid-Wales (Welsh Office 1964), the Highlands of Scotland (Central Office of Information 1957) and northern England (House 1965).

A continuous out-migration of young adults has a marked effect upon the social structure of the rural communities involved. According to Mitchell (1950a) a falling population, and the selective nature of the fall, contributes to a disintegration of traditional rural life. The removal of the relatively young, often the more able and articulate, reduces the number of potential leaders within the community, and this, allied to a falling and ageing population, makes the maintenance of a varied social life

Figure 4   USA: rural population change, 1950–60

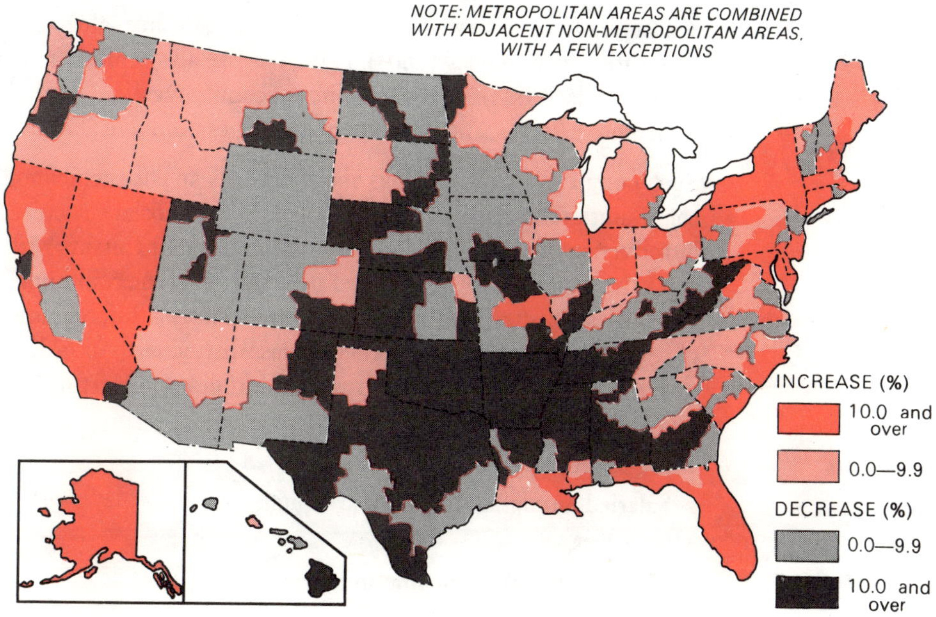

NOTE: METROPOLITAN AREAS ARE COMBINED
WITH ADJACENT NON-METROPOLITAN AREAS,
WITH A FEW EXCEPTIONS

INCREASE (%)

■ 10.0 and over

■ 0.0—9.9

DECREASE (%)

■ 0.0—9.9

■ 10.0 and over

Source: Beale (1964)

extremely difficult. Frankenberg (1957) has shown that small communities such as the one he studied in North Wales can sustain only a limited number of social organizations. In 'Pentrediwaith' during the 1950s only one major social organization could be sustained at any one time: during this period the football club declined and was replaced by the carnival as the major focus of community interest. Mitchell (1950b) has shown that in such ageing communities inter-personal contact is extremely strong; social life, however, becomes increasingly dependent on such relationships.

3.4   *Rural growth*   It was shown in 2.1 that, despite the general decline of rural population by migration, those areas adjacent to the major cities were today actually experiencing growth. Between 1951 and 1971 in England and Wales there was a considerable net in-migration into rural districts adjacent not only to the major metropolitan centres but also to small towns. Lewis (1970) and Maund (1974) have shown that there was considerable growth even around the towns of Aberystwyth and Hereford. The development of such population growth is due, on the one hand, to an out-migration by urban dwellers into the countryside and, on the other, to an increasing dependence of the rural dwellers on the town for employment. This increasing divorce of place of work from place of residence has been analysed by Lawton (1968) for the period since 1921. Essentially, it was shown that the length of the journey to work had increased to such an extent that virtually the whole of rural Britain was dependent upon an urban area for employment.

Lewis and Maund (1973) have claimed that such population changes may be conceived within a framework similar to the 'filtering' process discussed in 3.2. In this case the major source of the change is the aspirations and actions of the wealthier upper-middle classes. Their desire for rural residence and fuller inter-personal relationships initiates a move to the countryside. Since they have the finance and time to divorce work from residence by a considerable distance they become the leaders in the migration process. It can thus be supposed that, during the first stage, rural communities close to the city are invaded by these groups. At a second stage, as a result of improved transport facilities, the middle classes are added to these

45

communities, whilst the upper-middle classes move further out into the countryside in search of 'peace and tranquillity'. In other words, the suburbanization of the countryside is here viewed as a series of waves, on an analogy to Hägerstrand's 'innovation wave model' (1967). However, like all simplistic models this one ignores a number of factors, among which lines of communication, local planning policies, land ownership patterns, and developers' strategies need to be borne in mind.

Such population growth brings about not only an enlargement of the rural communities but also significant changes in their social structure. It results in an introduction of upper-middle- and middle-class inhabitants with different attitudes and values, and it creates a marked polarization of the community into 'newcomers' and the 'established'. Although these terms imply a differentiation based upon length of residence, they essentially reflect a class distinction. According to Pahl (1970 pp 66–8) the social structure of rural communities in Hertfordshire can be subdivided into additional groups:

1 Large property owners.

2 Salaried immigrants with some capital.

3 Spiralists.

4 Those with limited income and little capital.

5 The retired.

6 Council-house tenants.

7 Tied cottagers and other tenants.

8 Local tradesmen and owners of small businesses.

Initially, the 'newcomers' are the stimulus to the development of a whole series of new social organizations which involves the whole community. But, as the community grows and the 'newcomers' increase in number, there is a tendency for social activities to fragment along class lines. In other words, inter-personal contact becomes more difficult and personal assessment gives way to class as the basis of the identification of status.

4 Individual consequences of migration

The consequences of migration at an individual level are overwhelmingly concerned with the migrant's process of assimilation into a new community. A considerable amount of literature, probably beginning with W. I. Thomas and F. Znaniecki's classic study of the *Polish Peasant in Europe and America* (1958), has arisen to describe and analyse the nature of such assimilation. The majority of studies have been concerned with the prejudice and discrimination experienced by migrants, particularly their exclusion from certain spheres of activity and the problems created by the differences in norms, values, and customs between them and the host population. Such processes are vital in any understanding of the form of a number of surfaces, in particular those of social nature. A failure by migrants to assimilate into the host community accentuates contrasts within such a surface, conversely rapid assimilation can reduce such inequalities. Therefore, the process of assimilation plays a significant part in the development of social surfaces. Hence, a detailed study of assimilation is necessary.

4.1 Nature of assimilation

The assimilation of the migrant into the receiving community, according to Germani (1966), involves three, often interrelated, processes: adjustment, participation, and acculturation. In order to avoid terminological confusion such processes will be defined within this unit along the lines suggested by Germani:

(a) *Adjustment* – 'the manner in which the migrant is able to perform his roles in the various spheres of activity in which he participates' (p 163).

(b) *Participation* – 'how many and in which roles [he is] performing within the institutions, social groups, and various sections of the host community' (p 164).

(c) *Acculturation* – 'the process (and the degree) of acquisition and learning by the migrant of ways of behaviour (including roles, habits, attitudes, values, knowledge) of the receiving society' (p 164).

Table 2
The assimilation process

	Sub-process or condition	Type of Assimilation
1	Change of cultural patterns to those of host society.	Cultural or behavioural assimilation (acculturation).
2	Large-scale entrance into host society's primary groups (cliques, clubs etc.).	Structural assimilation (participation).
3	Large-scale inter-marriage.	Marital assimilation (amalgamation).
4	Development of sense of peoplehood based on host society.	Identificational assimilation (adjustment).
5	Absence of prejudice.	Attitude receptional assimilation.
6	Absence of discrimination.	Behaviour receptional assimilation.
7	Absence of value or power conflict.	Civic assimilation.

Source: Gordon (1964)

In his study of *Assimilation in American Life* (1964) Gordon goes a stage further by identifying the processes which bring about the assimilation of the migrant into the host society. By relating the processes involved ('sub-processes' or 'conditions') to different types of assimilation, he builds up a form of classification of the 'assimilation process' (Table 2).

Implicit within such a classification is the existence of a temporal component in the assimilation process. Gordon has hypothesized that the sequential nature of assimilation may take the following forms:

(i) 'Cultural assimilation, or acculturation, is likely to be the first of the types of assimilation to occur when a minority group arrives on the scene' (p 73).

(ii) 'Cultural assimilation, or acculturation, of the minority group may take place even when none of the other types of assimilation occurs simultaneously or later, and this condition of "acculturation only" may continue indefinitely' (p 77).

(iii) 'Once structural assimilation has occurred, either simultaneously with or subsequent to acculturation, all of the other types of assimilation will naturally follow' (p 81).

These hypotheses clearly emphasize the point that the components of assimilation do not necessarily all occur simultaneously. A given degree of adjustment (or participation, or acculturation) may be achieved in one sphere of activity but not in another. For example, a migrant may feel adjusted to the needs of his new job, and yet be unable to bear the psychological stress introduced by impersonal human relations in the new community. However, it is true that, at least with regard to certain spheres of activity, adjustment, participation, and acculturation will usually go together, though incongruities between different spheres of activities may be quite frequent.

After this brief outline of the process of assimilation it is now opportune to discuss the nature of the prejudice and discrimination experienced by migrants during their assimilation into the host society. This we shall do by means of a review of a series of case studies.

4.2   *Acculturation*   The acquisition of new cultural traits by the migrant may take place in various ways: it may consist of relatively superficial learning, or it may penetrate deeply into his personality. According to Price, it may be more or less internalized and the migrant may feel more or less involved in the new behaviour pattern. By internalization we may mean the process by which the trait becomes part of the personality of the individual, in which case a completely internalized behaviour pattern would be experienced as a spontaneous expression by the migrant himself. In the new setting the migrant is confronted with the need of acquiring new knowledge, and also new attitudes and new values. But in such re-socialization, he may achieve sometimes a sufficient, but not deeply experienced knowledge of the new behaviour patterns; and sometimes he may achieve a deeper level of internalization. In the field of attitudes and the values the resocialization may lead to a deep involvement and identification with the new pattern, to a very superficial acceptance, or to a more or less complete rejection. The recognition of such different forms and degrees of acculturation is sometimes of paramount importance (Price 1969 p 196).

Traditionally, studies of acculturation have emphasized the isolation of the newcomer from the host society as a result of differences in norms, values, and customs. As Louis Wirth wrote:

... as newer immigrant groups followed older waves, the latest comers increasingly became the objects of prejudice and discrimination on the part of natives and older immigrants alike ... Although the ethnic minorities in the United States suffer mainly from private prejudices rather than restrictive public policies, their path of assimilation is not without its serious obstacles ... Overanxiety about being accepted sometimes results in a pattern of conduct among minorities that provokes a defense reaction on the part of the dominant group; their defense reaction may take the form of rebuffs which are likely to accentuate minority consciousness and thus retard assimilation (Wirth 1945 p 64).

Similar forms of prejudice and discrimination in British cities have been revealed by a number of recent studies, in particular Richmond's (1973) analysis of race relations in Bristol. Of course, if such segregation involves a sufficient number of migrants they will form a distinctive minority group within the host society located within easily identifiable territorial limits.

4.3   *Adjustment*   Essentially, the concern here is with the migrant's ability to perform various roles without excessive or unbearable psychological stress. A number of studies have identified a relationship between migration and family disorganization, mental illness, delinquency, poverty, etc. The findings have stressed that migrants tend to have higher rates of these problems than do the host population. R. E. Park described the adjustment difficulties of the in-migrants to the American cities in the following manner:

... the enormous amount of delinquency, juvenile and adult, that exists today in the Negro communities in northern cities is due in part, though not entirely, to the fact that migrants are not able to accommodate themselves at once to a new and relatively strange environment. The same thing may be said of the immigrants from Europe, or of the younger generation of women who are just now entering in such large numbers into the new occupations and the freer life which the great cities offer them (Park 1925 p 37).

Similarly Bonilla described the *favelado* of Rio de Janeiro as being

... plagued by all the ills that beset his kind everywhere. As a group, the *favela* population is on the wrong side of every standard index of social disorganization whether it be illiteracy, malnutrition, disease, job instability, irregular sexual unions, alcoholism, criminal violence, or about any other on the familiar list (Bonilla 1961 p 72).

An explanation of such social disorganization is complex, and it is difficult to generalize. For example, Bogue has gone as far as to suggest four possible reasons as to why migrants are more prone to mental disorders than non-migrants. Briefly, they are:

1 '... a lack of a supportive receiving population that favours rapid and easy social adjustments lead to mental stress and disorder. When the migrant enters a family situation or an ethnic community where he is given personal nurture, rates of mental illness are low.'

2 'Aggravated hostility, prejudice, and highly inconsistent behaviour on the part of the receiving community may be conducive to mental disorders.'

3 'In some situations migrants leave their homeland gladly and without great mental stress, but in others their movement is forced by tragic circumstances, so that the separation is a very traumatic one.'

4 'In some instances migration involves comparatively little change for the migrant, he simply continues his former pattern of life in a similar but different place. Other forms of migration may involve a dramatic transition that requires a complete reorganization of the personality' (Bogue 1969 p 800).

The above may be an over-elaborate way of stating the obvious: i.e. that the mental health of migrants is a function of the amount of stress they must undergo in the process of separating themselves from their community of origin and of gaining the status of accepted members of their community of destination. It is also very plausible to suppose that it is often persons in a state of deep anxiety and stress who will seek to migrate in an effort to resolve their problems. A similar pattern of relationship exists between migration and other forms of adjustment.

4.4 Participation

In a study of a migrant's participation in the social and economic structure of the host society it is necessary to distinguish at least three different dimensions. First, how many, and which, roles is the migrant performing within the institutions, social groups and various sectors of the receiving community? Second, how efficiently are such roles being performed by the migrant, particularly as viewed from the standpoint of the receiving institutions and groups and of the values of the receiving society? And third, how do the social groups and institutions of the receiving society react with regard to the migrants and their participation? Often in this context the term *integration* is used to refer specifically to the degree of accepted and/or non-conflictual participation. Thus, the degree of participation of the migrant in the various social groups and institutions of the host society, can really be assessed only when it is compared with that of the native population. Although a migrant may be participating very fully within the host community, he may still not be fully adjusted or acculturated. The nature of differential rates of participation has been revealed by a number of studies. For example, Zimmer (1970) has carried out a detailed study of migrant participation in an American Midwestern urban community (population 20,000). By use of such indices as membership of formal organizations, offices held in formal organizations, and registration to vote, Zimmer revealed lower rates of participation among the migrants than among the native population. However, the migrants' rates of participation increased with their length of residence in the host community, and the greater the similarity of the migrants' social and economic background to that of the receiving society, the more quickly they came to participate in the activities of that society: for example, it was found that urban migrants tended to enter the activities of the community more rapidly than farm migrants. Such conclusions are readily supported by a wide variety of other studies of migrant participation.

4.5 Stages of assimilation

There have been many attempts to identify the stages which an individual goes through during his assimilation into a host society. Broadly speaking, there are two major theories – the 'melting-pot' and 'ethnic-pluralities' theories – which attempt to explain the assimilation process, and in many ways these correspond to the 'filtering' and 'segregation' processes discussed in 3.2. Essentially, the first theory looks towards the eventual conformity of the immigrant within the host community; the second assumes that differences will harden into permanent distinct groups. A wide variety of sequences generalizing the process of assimilation have been described, and since these have been well documented elsewhere (Price 1969), reference will here be made only to two examples which stand midway between the two theories.

According to Duncan (1933), Galitzi (1929) and Hitti (1924) the assimilation process involves three generations. The stages these writers identify may be summarized as follows:

(a) *First generation* – although a few immigrants assimilate completely, the overwhelming majority adopt only a limited number of the host society's social and economic values, and so form ethnic groups and institutions to maintain their original culture.

(b) *Bridge generation* – there is a tendency for this generation to preserve the 'old' culture at home as a result of parental pressure and to acquire the 'host' culture outside the home, so forming a mixed set of values and a dual culture.

(c) *Assimilated generation* – under pressure from the host society this generation rejects the 'old' culture and adopts all the values and customs of the 'host' culture. Thus the process of assimilation is complete.

There has been considerable criticism of these stages by a number of scholars (see Price 1969). Some have argued that during the third generation there is a tendency to revert back to the 'old' culture, whilst others, basing themselves upon American evidence, have emphasized the tendency for ethnic differences to wane within the triple contexts of Protestantism, Catholicism, and Judaism. As a result of these criticisms a further modification to the process of assimilation has been suggested by Glazer and Moynihan (1963) along the following lines:

(a) *First stage* – the creation of ethnic groups and organizations but a gradual disappearance of ethnic culture and language.

(b) *Second stage* – beginning of the transformation of the ethnic groups into 'interest' groups distinguished by colour and religion, by attitudes to education, politics, and family life.

(c) *Third stage* – the disappearance of the ethnic groups into divisions of colour and religion.

Unfortunately, the majority of studies of assimilation are based upon the North American experience where ethnic difference is the major source of differentiation. However, it could be argued that in any society the same processes operate, and that differences are only a matter of detail. In addition, it appears that the greater the initial differences, the greater the problem of assimilation; and where racial prejudice is significant then both the 'melting-pot' and 'ethnic-pluralities' processes are operative, even during the latter stages.

5   Conclusion   This unit has discussed and attempted to explain the important cultural, political, and social consequences of migration at three societal scales. If such an approach is adopted, it becomes clear that any major societal or regional shift of population has marked consequences for the communities and individuals involved. The nature of the social, political, and cultural difficulties experienced by individuals and social groups, as a consequence of migration, may well lead to the questioning of the widely-held view that large-scale mobility is of considerable benefit for the regions involved. Certainly such consequences need to be taken into account in determining priorities in any form of regional development.

Self-assessment Questions   SAQ 1   Differentiate between migration as a dependent and independent variable.

SAQ 2   How would you state the case for and against seasonal migration in West Africa?

SAQ 3   Outline the major stages in the concentration of population.

SAQ 4   How can a socio-economic surface change?

SAQ 5   In what ways can the encouragement of temporary labour immigrants in Western Europe be viewed as a short-sighted policy?

SAQ 6 Why is the classical theory of migration and urban growth now considered inadequate?

SAQ 7 In what ways is Rex and Moore's concept of 'housing classes' an inadequate explanation of residential segregation?

SAQ 8 Why do areas peripheral to towns and cities experience a population growth?

SAQ 9 What is the effect of such population growth upon the social structure of the communities involved?

SAQ 10 Define acculturation, participation, and adjustment.

SAQ 11 Why do certain migrants have higher rates of social disorganization than non-migrants?

SAQ 12 Distinguish between the 'melting-pot' and 'ethnic-pluralities' theories of assimilation.

Answers   SAQ 1 As a dependent variable migration is a response to social, political, economic and cultural change within society. As an independent variable it can initiate change itself.

SAQ 2 *For:*   Seasonal migration has permitted West African countries to experience more rapid economic growth than might otherwise have been possible; it has strengthened the economic infrastructure through the need to develop roads and transportation facilities; the cash economy is beginning to spread to the rural districts.
Against: Temporary migration makes labour productivity lower than it would be if the same labour force were permanent; it means the disruption of agricultural production and of the authority structure in rural areas; it discourages the establishment of a permanent industrial labour force; it may lead to social problems in recipient areas where migrants of different origins are brought together.

SAQ 3 According to Gibbs such a population redistribution takes place in *five* distinct stages: (1) the early growth of cities; (2) cities grow faster than rural communities; (3) rural communities experience an absolute decline; (4) the smaller cities also experience a decline; (5) the beginnings of an opposite trend take place, the out-migration of individuals from the places of population concentration, the major cities, to adjacent and more distant places, thus initiating a change towards a more even spatial distribution of population.

SAQ 4 Such a surface can change as a result of the redistribution of population, the redistribution of social groups, a shift in the distribution of the size and structure of the labour force, and the development of further social and economic inequalities consequent upon such movements.

SAQ 5 Two ways may be suggested. First, an overdependence upon such labour may induce economic difficulties for Western Europe if stricter emigration policies are introduced by the native countries. Second, socio-political conflict between the native workers and the immigrants may develop. The increasing number of immigrants and their desire to better themselves is seen as a threat by the natives.

SAQ 6 Two major reasons are involved. First, the pattern of migration envisaged by the theory does not correspond with reality, since different groups of in-migrants tend to move directly into different zones within the city. Second, it is clearly apparent that not all migrants are able to achieve social and spatial mobility.

SAQ 7   According to this concept the discrimination experienced by the immigrant is interpreted as discrimination against him solely as a *newcomer* and a member of a particular housing class. However, such an analysis fails to explain adequately why some migrants to the city eventually move from the inner city while others find themselves confined to a perpetual 'ghetto'. Increasingly, empirical evidence seems to point towards *racial* prejudice as the major factor preventing the geographical dispersion and social mobility of some migrant groups.

SAQ 8   The development of such a population growth is due, on the one hand, to an out-migration by urban dwellers into the countryside, and on the other, to an increasing dependence of the rural dwellers on the town for employment.

SAQ 9   Such a population growth brings about not only an enlargement of the rural communities but also significant changes in their social structure. It results in an introduction of upper-middle- and middle-class inhabitants with different attitudes and values, and creates a marked polarization of the community into 'newcomers' and the 'established'.

SAQ 10   *Acculturation* is the process of acquiring the ways of behaviour of a society on the part of a migrant; *participation* is the number of roles a migrant performs within the host society; *adjustment* is the manner in which the migrant is able to perform his roles.

SAQ 11   Bogue has suggested four reasons. First, a lack of supportive receiving population; second, hostility on the part of the receiving population; third, the separation from the native home can in certain instances be traumatic; and fourth, the new environment may involve a complete reorganization of the personality.

SAQ 12   'Melting-pot' theory assumes the eventual conformity of the immigrant within the host community; 'ethnic-pluralities' theory assumes that differences will harden into permanent distinct groups.

References   ALDKOGIUS, M. (1970) 'Population Change and Urban Growth', *Geografiska Annaler*, 52B, pp 131–40.

ARUNCHALAM, B., PHADKE, V.S. and DESHPANDE, (1972) 'South Kolaba: A Study in Demographic Characteristics', paper presented at the Indo-British Seminar, Delhi.

BARCLAY, G. W. (1958) *Techniques of Population Analysis*, New York, John Wiley.

BEALE, C. L. (1964) 'Rural Depopulation in the United States: Some Consequences of Agricultural Adjustments', *Demography*, 1, pp 264–72.

BERG, E. (1965) 'The Economics of the Migrant Labour System', in H. Kuper (ed), *Urbanization and Migration in West Africa*, Los Angeles, University of California Press.

BOGUE, D. J. (1969) *The Principles of Demography*, London, John Wiley.

BONILLA, F. (1970) 'Rio's Favelas', in W. Mangin (ed) *Peasants in Cities: Readings in the Anthropology of Urbanization*, Boston, Houghton Mifflin Co.

CALDWELL, J. C. (1961) 'Migration and Urbanization', in W. Birmingham *et al*, *A Study of Contemporary Ghana*, Vol. 2, London, George Allen and Unwin.

CALDWELL, J. C. (1968) 'Determinants of Rural-Urban Migration in Ghana', *Population Studies*, 22, pp 361–75.

CENTRAL OFFICE OF INFORMATION (1957) *Depopulation and Rural Life in Scotland*, London, H.M.S.O.

COATES, B. E. and RAWSTRON, E. M. (1966) 'Opportunity and Affluence', *Geography*, 51, pp 1–15.

COMPTON, P. A. (1969) 'Internal Migration and Population Change in Hungary between 1959 and 1965', *Transactions of the Institute of British Geographers*, 47, pp 111–30.

DAVIES, W. K. and LEWIS, G. J. (1974) 'The Social Patterning of a British City: The Case of Leicester 1966', *Tijdschrift Voor Economische en Sociale Geografie*, 65, pp 97–109.

DUNCAN, H. G. (1933) *Immigration and Assimilation*, New York, John Wiley.

EISENSTADT, S. N. (1954), *The Absorption of Immigrants*, London, Routledge and Kegan Paul.

FRANKENBERG, R. (1957) *The Village on the Border*, London, Cohen and West.

GANS, H. J. (1962) *The Urban Villagers*, New York, Oxford University Press.

GALITZI, C. A. (1929) *A Study of Assimilation among the Roumanians in the United States*, New York, John Wiley.

GERMANI, G. (1966) 'Migration and Acculturation', in *Handbook for Social Research in Urban Areas*, New York, UNESCO, pp 159–78.

GIBBS, J. P. (1963) 'The Evolution of Population Concentration', *Economic Geography*, 39, pp 340–50.

GLAZER, N. and MOYNIHAN, D. (1963) *Beyond the Melting Pot*, Cambridge, Mass., M.I.T. Press.

GOLDSCHREIDER, C. (1971) *Population, Modernization, and Social Structure*, Boston, Little, Brown.

GORDON, M. M. (1964) *Assimilation in American Life*, New York, Oxford University Press.

GUARDIAN, THE (1973), September 4th.

HÄGERSTRAND, T. (1967) *Innovation Diffusion as a Spatial Process*, Chicago, University of Chicago Press.

HALL, C. B. and SMITH, R. A. (1968) 'Socio-economic Patterns of England and Wales', *Urban Studies*, 5, pp 59–66.

HITTI, P. K. (1924) *The Syrians in America*, New York, George H. Doran Co.

HOUSE, J. W. (1965) *Rural North-East England: 1951–61*, Department of Geography, University of Newcastle-upon-Tyne, Papers on Migration and Mobility, No 1.

JANSEN, C. J. (1969) 'Some Sociological Aspects of Migration', in J. A. Jackson (ed) *Migration*, Cambridge, Cambridge University Press.

LAWTON, R. (1968) 'The Journey to Work in Britain: Some Trends and Problems', *Regional Studies*, 2, pp 27–40.

LEWIS, G. J. (1970) 'Suburbanization in Rural Wales: A Case Study', in H. Carter and W. K. Davies (eds) *Urban Essays: Studies in the Geography of Wales*, London, Longman.

LEWIS, G. J. and MAUND, D. J. (1973) *The Urbanization of the Countryside: A Framework for Analysis*, Department of Geography, University of Leicester, Discussion Paper.

LIND, H. (1969) 'Internal Migration in Britain', in J. A. Jackson (ed) *Migration*, Cambridge, Cambridge University Press.

MATRAS, J. (1973) *Populations and Societies*, Englewood Cliffs, New Jersey, Prentice-Hall.

MAUND, D. J. (1974) *Suburbanization in Rural Herefordshire*, unpublished M.Phil thesis, University of Leicester.

MITCHELL, G. D. (1950a) 'Social Disintegration in a Rural Community', *Human Relations*, 3, pp 279–306.

MITCHELL, G. D. (1950b) 'Depopulation and Rural Social Structure', *Sociological Review*, 42, pp 11–24.

OSBORNE, R. H. (1955) 'Internal Migration in England and Wales 1951', *Advancement of Science*, 12, pp 137–62.

OSBORNE, R. H. (1964) 'Migration Trends of England and Wales 1901–51', *Geografia Polonica*, 3, pp 137–62.

PAHL, R. E. (1970) *Patterns of Urban Life*, London, Longman.

PARK, R. E. (1925) *Human Communities*, Glencoe, Free Press.

PARK, R. E., BURGESS, E. W. and MCKENZIE, R. (1925) *The City*, Chicago, University of Chicago Press.

PRESSAT, R. (1972) *Demographic Analysis : Methods, Results, Applications*, Chicago, Aldine.

PRICE, C. (1969) 'The Study of Assimilation', in J. A. Jackson (ed) *Migration*, Cambridge, Cambridge University Press.

REES, P. H. (1970) 'Concepts of Social Space: Towards an Urban Social Geography', in B. J. L. Berry and F. E. Horton (eds) *Geographic Perspectives on Urban Systems*, New York, Prentice-Hall.

REX, J. A. and MOORE, R. (1967) *Race, Community and Conflict*, London, Oxford University Press.

REX, J. A. (1968) 'The Sociology of a Zone in Transition', in R. E. Pahl (ed) *Readings in Urban Sociology*, Oxford, Pergamon.

RICHMOND, A. H. (1973) *Migration and Race Relations in an English City*, London, Oxford University Press.

ROGERS, A. (1968) *Matrix Analysis of Interregional Population Growth and Distribution*, Berkeley, University of California Press.

ROGERS, E. M. (1962) *Diffusion of Innovations*, Glencoe, Free Press.

ROSE, H. M. (1972) *The Black Ghetto*, New York, McGraw-Hill.

SHRYOCK, H. S. (1964) *Population Mobility within the United States*, Chicago, Community and Family Study Centre.

SKINNER, E. (1966) 'Labour Migration and its Relationship to Socio–Cultural Change in Mossi Society', in I. Wallerstein (ed) *Social Change*, London, John Wiley.

SUNDAY TIMES, THE (1973) 'The Slave Workers of Europe', July 22nd, pp 62–63.

TAEUBER, K. E. and TAEUBER, G. F. (1964) 'The Negro as an Immigrant Group: Recent Trends in Racial and Ethnic Segregation in Chicago', *American Journal of Sociology*, 64, pp 374–82.

THOMAS, W. I. and ZNANIECKI, F. (1958) *The Polish Peasant in Europe and America*, New York, Owen.

WARD, D. (1971) *Cities and Immigrants : A Geography of Change in Nineteenth Century America*, New York, Oxford University Press.

WAUGH, M. (1969) 'The Changing Distribution of Professional and Managerial Manpower in England and Wales between 1961 and 1966', *Regional Studies*, 3, pp 157–69.

WELSH OFFICE, THE (1964) *Depopulation in Mid-Wales*, London, H.M.S.O.

WIRTH, L. (1945) 'The problem of minority groups', in R. Linton (ed) *The Science of Man in the World Crisis*, New York, Columbia University Press.

ZIMMER, B. G. (1970) 'Participation of Migrants in Urban Structures', reprinted in C. J. Jansen (ed) *Readings in the Sociology of Migration*, Oxford, Pergamon.

Acknowledgements Grateful acknowledgement is made to the following sources for material used in this unit:

Figures

Figures 1 and 2 : Department of Geography, The University of Reading for M. Waugh in *Regional Studies*, 3, pp 160 and 169, 1969; *Figure 3 :* The Sunday Times; *Figure 4 :* Population Association of America for C. L. Beale in *Demography*, 1, 267, 1964.

Tables

Table 1 : Cambridge University Press for J. A. Jackson (ed)., *Migration*, 1969; *Table 2 :* Oxford University Press for M. M. Gordon, *Assimilation in American Life*.

55

Unit 11
Economic complexes

Prepared by Charles Choguill

Contents

		Page
1	Introduction	61
1.1	Aims	61
1.2	Objectives	61
2	Growth factors at a location	61
2.1	Micro-aspects of macro-growth theories	61
2.2	Internal sources of growth	62
2.2.1	Localization economies	63
2.2.2	Urbanization economies	63
3	Analysing the sectoral transmission of growth	64
3.1	Introduction	64
3.2	Input-output analysis	64
3.3	Industrial complex analysis	67
4	Spatial spread of economic impulses	70
4.1	Introduction	70
4.2	Interfirm linkages as a mechanism for spread	70
4.2.1	Empirical observations of the linkage mechanics	71
4.2.2	Linkage analysis in planning complexes	73
4.2.3	Process analysis and complexes	74
4.3	Competition for resources as a mechanism for spread	75
4.3.1	Competition for land and rent	75
4.3.2	Competition for labour	75
4.4	Diffusion	76
5	Growth pole theory as a synthesis of agglomeration and transmission	79
5.1	The concept of growth poles	79
5.2	Prerequisites of a growth pole	79
5.2.1	Dominance	80
5.2.2	Polarization	82
5.2.3	Spread effects	83
5.2.4	Polarization and spread effects combined	84
5.3	An intuitive evaluation of growth poles	84
6	Case studies of the growth pole concept	86
6.1	The case of Lacq	86
6.2	The case of Lannion	88
7	Conclusion	89
	Self-assessment Questions	90
	References	93

1 Introduction

In the preceding units of Block III, emphasis has been placed upon the ways by which the economic and social structure of a region may be conceived in terms of economic and social surfaces. Given the dynamic nature of regional development, it should not be surprising to learn that these surfaces will change over time. These changes are the result of a number of factors, some of which have been considered in earlier units. As observed in Unit 8, firms move from one location to another. The factors underlying the migration of people were considered in Unit 9, while in Unit 10, the consequences of this migration were examined.

In the present unit, the possible effects of new economic activity at a location are analysed: the type of new activity that may result from the migration of firms or from the creation of new enterprises. Furthermore, it is necessary to note that many types of activities, like people, have a natural tendency to congregate at specific locations. This tendency to form economic complexes is the result of a number of underlying causal factors, some of which have already been noted in Block II, where alternative theories of regional growth were introduced.

1.1 Aims

The aim of this unit is to focus upon the locations whose economic activities act as a driving force of economic growth. Industrial enterprises have historically played a key role in such growth processes. Therefore, the interdependence of industries will form the central core of the analysis. We will also examine some of the methods used to analyse the transmission of growth from one economic sector to another and from one geographical location to another. Although these techniques of analysis are complex, the intuitive concepts upon which they are based are fairly easy to understand. Therefore, where possible, we will concentrate on those underlying ideas.

1.2 Objectives

After reading this unit you should:

— Be able to explain why certain kinds of economic activities tend to locate close to one another.

— Understand the meaning of agglomeration, as well as the various types of economies that might be expected to result from such groupings.

— Understand how growth can be transmitted from one economic sector to another.

— Understand how growth can be transmitted from one location to another.

— Be able to explain the meaning of the growth pole concept, as well as give the conditions that are necessary for a successful growth pole.

— Understand why growth poles at some locations have been successful, while others have not.

2 Growth factors at a location

You have already seen in Unit 4 how regional growth might be the result of factors which are external, or exogenous, to the region. According to the economic base theory, export activity is the primary determinant of regional income. As regional exports rise, specialization would be expected to occur in the export-orientated industries. According to that theory, incomes within the region would also rise, resulting in the development of new economic activities which may not necessarily be export orientated. These service activities are the direct result of the increase in regional exports. This relationship between income and exports has been formally stated in Equation 2.8 of Unit 4, where the regional multiplier was defined as the relationship between export income and net regional income.

2.1 Micro-aspects of macro-growth theories

Up to this point, these concepts have been used in their macro-sense; that is, as a method of viewing the increases in income that have been generated by the regional economy as a whole. In dealing with economic complexes, however, primary emphasis is directed not to the regional economy in total, but to the role of the firm and the relationships between firms. The macro-concepts of Block II can readily be extended to include the type of micro-analysis that is central to this unit. If there is an increase in the demand for the products of a firm, economic theory tells us that the reaction of the firm will vary according to the length of time considered in the analysis. In the short run, where all factors of production are assumed to be fixed, increased production can only arise as a result of increased productivity of the labour force, itself perhaps a result of better internal organization, or more intensive use of existing productive equipment, or perhaps the result of an increase in overtime work by the existing work force. As the time period constraint is relaxed, production levels can be still further augmented. Initially, it would be expected that the labour force hired by the firm would be increased, leading perhaps to round-the-clock production. In the long run, where all factors of production are viewed as variable, new capital equipment and possibly even new buildings would be constructed to increase output.

The ramification from this increase in the firm's output as a result of exogenous demand for the product should be apparent. In short run analysis, the increased revenue obtained for the firm's product may be re-spent in its own locality. The revenue may be used to finance the overtime production activity, to obtain greater amounts of raw material, to pay off existing debt or to provide the basis for future investment. A part of the increased wages paid for the overtime work of the labour force will be added to the income stream of that community. This will result in increased purchases by retailers and thus still more income will be generated which again increases potential purchasing power and leads to a further rise in income levels. Economic base theory suggests that the upper limit on the increase in incomes will be dependent upon the leakages of income out of the economy such as the amount paid for non-local taxes and for imports from other regions (a more detailed consideration of the regional multiplier was presented in Unit 4, Section 2.2).

In the longer run, a similar pattern is to be expected. As new workers are hired, perhaps from the ranks of the locally unemployed, further consumption expenditure will result. If the new labour is the result of migration from another region, the consumption expenditure will represent a shift from one region to another. Construction of plant and equipment will lead to further increases in local economic activity, constrained again, however, by leakages for imports. New firms might be created to meet the consumption demands of the increased work force, in a manner analogous to the service-oriented firms in traditional economic base theory. Further urban services might be demanded, and provided, leading to still further increases in employment, income and demand.

Each element of these increases can readily be included in the micro-version of economic base ratios, relating increases in demand for the firm's product from exogenous sources with increases in local income resulting from direct and indirect increases in employment. Certain of these concepts will be developed further in later sections, as the concept of the multiplier plays an important role in the analysis which follows.

2.2 Internal sources of growth

It should be apparent that not all sources of regional growth are caused by factors external to the region (for example, look back to Unit 1, Part B, Section 2). In fact, in this unit, we are particularly interested in those factors which might be called endogenous, that is, factors originating within the region in question. In Unit 5, you were introduced to certain of these factors, particularly investments in regional infrastructure, which might make the growth of one region more likely than another. If such regional investments successfully stimulate growth, hence changing the nature of the cost surfaces, there are strong forces which might well lead to a situation in which firms locate in proximity to one another, or *agglomerate*, at some point in space. Such investment at a point in space might also be expected to stimulate activity among firms already located at that point. This agglomeration, and the resulting economies, are often treated under two separate headings: localization economies and urbanization economies.

| 2.2.1 | *Localization economies* | *Localization economies* include the savings that might result from agglomeration of various firms of the same industrial type locating near to one another. A crucial factor in this definition is the industrial classification system that is used. A broad definition, perhaps consisting of all manufacturing enterprises, would not be of as much analytical value as some finer classification such as part of manufacturing, based perhaps on the nature of the sector's predominant input (e.g. metal-working industries). |

Let us suppose that a steel mill has been established at some location to take advantage of raw material supplies, such as iron ore, coal and limestone. At some later stage, steel fabricating industries might be attracted to the location of the steel mill. As you know, such firms might migrate from other locations, or establish themselves at that location for the first time. Given either source, the firms will be attracted to the steel mill for the same reasons: the probability of a low-cost source of material inputs. As workers are trained for jobs in the metal fabricating industry, other metal fabricating firms will view this location as a source of skilled labour. Such a ready supply of essential labour means savings to the new firms. Sub-contracting among the firms might be a further source of potential economy that might be exploited.

Ideally, the analysis of localization economies should include some assessment of the level of savings reaped by the firms. Unfortunately, such information is extremely difficult for the analyst to obtain, and may even be unknown to the firms involved. Florence (1948) has, nevertheless, suggested a measure which at least identifies those sectors that tend to agglomerate and would be expected to profit from localization economies. This measure of the *location quotient*, L_Q, might be defined as

$$L_Q = \frac{N_{i,r}/N_{t,r}}{N_{i,n}/N_{t,n}}$$

where

$N_{i,r}$ represents employment in industrial sector i of area r,
$N_{t,r}$ is total industrial employment in area r,
$N_{i,n}$ is total employment in industrial sector i of the nation, and
$N_{t,n}$ represents total industrial employment in the nation.

As you can see, the location quotient is simply the comparison of two percentages, one giving the percentage of employment in some sector for the area, the second giving the similar percentage for some reference area, such as the nation. If the share of employment in a particular sector was greater than the nation's, the location quotient for that industry would be greater than unity. If less, it would be smaller than unity.

| 2.2.2 | *Urbanization economies* | *Urbanization economies* are distinguished from localization economies in that they refer to savings that might be derived from all firms in all industrial types at a single location. It should be apparent that urbanization economies are largely the result of urban growth. As a city grows in size it is to be expected that the range of services available to industry will increase, and the higher level of demand will allow specialization leading to lower costs to all firms. The costs to the individual firms is shared out among more and more enterprises, resulting in a reduced expense for each. For example, at higher levels of demand, public services, such as utilities, obtain economies of scale, a situation which would result in lower charges. An abundant labour force is more readily available, reducing training costs for any individual firm. Banking and credit facilities are increasingly likely to be present in such a growing urban situation. Each of these factors, shared as they are among an |

increasing number of firms, results in economies to each individual firm in the urban complex.

Although, as in the case of localization economies, the actual level of savings that might be obtained from this type of grouping together is difficult to quantify, a similar measure of the extent of agglomeration can be estimated by an *urbanization quotient*, U_Q, which could be defined as

$$U_Q = \frac{N_{t,r}/N_{T,r}}{N_{t,n}/N_{T,n}}$$

where

$N_{t,r}$ represents total industrial employment in area r,

$N_{T,r}$ is total employment in all sectors of area r,

$N_{t,n}$ is total industrial employment in the nation, and

$N_{T,n}$ is total employment in all sectors of the nation.

As with the location quotient, this measure increases in magnitude as the local area becomes increasingly specialized in the industrial sectors deemed relevant for the analysis of urbanization economies.

3 Analysing the sectoral transmission of growth

3.1 Introduction

As you have noted in the preceding section, the height of points on the production cost surface (that is, the level of production costs at different locations) can be reduced by the development of agglomeration economies. However, there are other kinds of surfaces which are also relevant to the firm as well, such as market potential surfaces (see Unit 7, Section 2.1.3). The technical, as well as spatial arrangement of enterprises can affect both costs and revenues, and hence profits. By examining the nature of technical relationships, we can, at the same time, gain still further insight into the importance of the spatial relationship.

There are at least two major techniques of regional analysis that can be used to analyse the technical relationships between sectors and activities. An understanding of these models provides further information on the nature of the intersectoral transmission of economic activity. The first of these is input-output analysis, a technique that, as you have already seen in Unit 4, can be used to examine trade flows among regions. The second technique, industrial complex analysis, is useful for detailed examination of the economic flows within a group of activities at a single location, including the quantitative assessment of certain factors associated with agglomeration. An understanding of these two techniques should yield considerable insight into the methods by which the nature of economic surfaces can be transformed as the number of interfirm linkages increases.

3.2 Input-output analysis

The basis of input-output analysis, which was developed by Leontief at Harvard University in the 1930s and 1940s, is the interdependencies that exist among the various firms that make up an economy. With an input-output transaction table, it is possible to measure the technical linkages that exist between industrial sectors. Furthermore, it is possible to determine which sectors are most dependent upon the demand of final consumers (such as households) as contrasted with those which are dependent upon industrial demand (which implies further processing of a commodity). Finally, as you shall see, the input-output framework is a valuable aid in quantitatively estimating the impact of individual events upon the economy.

Let us suppose that a rather complete industrial census has been made of a regional economy, revealing the characteristics as shown in Table 1.

The information contained in the table gives the total value (in £ millions) of the transactions among three broadly based economic sectors over the course of some time period, say one year. Consider the first row of numbers in the table giving the data for the agricultural sector. Farmers sold £20 million worth of their output to other farmers, perhaps in the form of feed grains to livestock producers, breeding stock to ranchers, etc. The farmers also sold £15 million of their produce to manufacturers, including such transactions as wheat to flour mills, fruit to canners, etc. They sold £5 million of their output to the trade and services sector. The final sale of the agricultural sector was to what is sometimes referred to as final demand. *Final demand* simply indicates sales to those destinations not already considered. This includes sales to individual consumers, taxes paid to government, export sales and new investment.

Table 1   Hypothetical input-output transactions table

Purchases by: Sales by:	Agriculture	Manufacturing	Trade & services	Final demand	Total
Agriculture	20	15	5	10	50
Manufacturing	10	50	15	25	100
Trade & services	5	10	15	10	40
Value added	15	25	5	5	50
TOTAL	50	100	40	50	240

The input-output transactions table has been compared with a double-entry book-keeping system. Therefore, if we looked down the agricultural column, we could determine which sectors provided inputs to the agricultural sector. As we have already noted, £20 million worth of these inputs came from the agricultural sector itself, while £10 million came from the manufacturing sector and £5 million from trade and services. The final set of inputs came from a sector which collectively is labelled value added. The *value added* sector is analogous to final demand; it includes inputs by labour from households, from government, imports for production and depreciation of the regional stock of capital. You should note that the total value of inputs into the agricultural sector, £50 million, is exactly equal to the output value of that sector. In input-output analysis the entire value of output must be imputed to some other sector, hence there are no unaccounted-for profits or losses as might exist in a traditional accounting system for the firm.

For analytical purposes, the input-output analyst converts these gross flows among sectors to a table of *technical coefficients*. This technical coefficient is defined as the value of the flow between any two sectors divided by the total value of output of the receiving sector. Consider the technical coefficient relating sales by the manufacturing sector to purchases by the agricultural sector. As you can see by the transactions table, the value of this flow is £10 million. Dividing this figure by the value of output in the agricultural sector, £50 million, the appropriate technical coefficient is .200. In Table 2, the technical coefficients for each of the industrial sectors are presented.

The technical coefficients reveal the value of inputs (in pence) from a sector required to produce £1 in final output by the producing sector. From this definition, as well as the principle of imputing the value of all sales to some particular input sector, it is apparent that the value of inputs in any column of the matrix cannot exceed unity. It should be noted that in this form of the input-output model, technical coefficients are only computed for the interindustry sectors, that is, for inputs into further industrial processing. Both the final demand and value added sectors are assumed to be governed by factors which are external to the interindustry processes. Government demand, for example, might be a part of a counter-cyclical economic policy that is in no way associated with the technical relationships within the economy. On the other hand, the interindustry transactions for which technical coefficients have been computed are strictly determined by these relationships.

Table 2   Hypothetical table of technical coefficients

Sales by: \ Purchases by:	Agriculture	Manufacturing	Trade & services
Agriculture	.400	.150	.125
Manufacturing	.200	.500	.375
Trade & services	.100	.100	.375

To this point, the input–output table has been used exclusively as a descriptive device. In the form of Table 1, the input–output table could be used as a regional accounting system to trace the commodity flows among various regional industries and for export. From such a table, one can determine the importance of interindustry linkages, as well as the importance of intra-industry coefficients (e.g., agriculture to agriculture). The hypothetical example we have used has been highly aggregated, masking vital relationships that could be taking place, and would be revealed if a finer classification of industrial inputs and outputs were available. Yet, even in the largest tables, such as the 500 sector table constructed for the Philadelphia area of the United States (Isard and Langford, 1971), the information on relationships between individual firms is lost.

In order to use the input–output technique for projection and forecasting purposes, it is necessary to consider certain assumptions upon which the model is based. Perhaps the most important of these assumptions is the linear nature of the relationships. In a linear model, such as input–output, it is assumed that if a sector wishes to double its output, this can only be done by doubling all inputs.

Another important assumption of the formulation we have examined is that it is a static model, that is, it does not include provision for structural change. In effect, it is like a photograph of the economy at one point in time. Generally, input–output analysts assume that the technical coefficients are constant over short periods of time, say five years, allowing for the use of such a static model to be used for forecasting purposes.

In summary, input–output represents one technique that is based on the technical linkages that exist among industries. Despite sweeping assumptions, the model is useful both as a method of describing how the regional economy operates and in determining the impact of a change in its structure. Although the high degree of sector aggregation may tend to hide vital linkages that could conceivably be exploited in the development process, input–output still ranks as one of the most popular techniques for the analysis of regional economic structure.

3.3 Industrial complex analysis

Whereas the input-output technique considers the relationships that exist within an economy as a whole, whether it be a regional or national economy, the industrial complex model can be designed for much more detailed analysis of activity at an isolated location. While input-output analysis focuses upon the interrelationships among broad sectors, industrial complex analysis can be used to examine the linkages among activities, or processes, within an agglomeration. Industrial complexes can be based on any one of a number of basic industries: the iron and steel industry, the petrochemical industries, food-processing industries, aero-space related industries, the textile industry and so on. In these complexes, inputs for one productive unit might be obtained from a neighbouring firm, sub-contracts might be let to smaller enterprises and marketing facilities might be shared among firms, situations which would clearly affect the cost surfaces affecting the components of the complex.

The principles involved in industrial complex analysis can perhaps best be illustrated by an example of its use. Whereas the input-output model can be used either as a descriptive tool or as a method of forecasting, the industrial complex model is basically a planning technique. An entrepreneur can use the model to evaluate the economic feasibility of a set of interrelated activities.

The best documented case study illustrating the use of industrial complex analysis concerns the establishment of a petrochemical complex in Puerto Rico (Isard, Schooler and Vietorisz, 1959). At the time this complex was planned, the Puerto Rican economy was relatively underdeveloped. One of the few resources that the island possessed was an abundant supply of unskilled labour. Puerto Rico did possess, however, certain historical and locational advantages. It was able to sell its output in the United States market free of import duties. Furthermore, it had the advantage of being located within proximity of oil tanker routes moving from Venezuela to the United States. The problem in complex planning, then, became one of determining an economic way to link together these advantages.

As you may be aware, petroleum can be used in the production of a wide range of various products, ranging from fuels and lubricating oils to various gaseous products, such as benzene, butylene, butane, propylene, propane, ethylene, ethane, methane and hydrogen. By further conversion of these various products, nitric acid, ammonium nitrate, urea and fertilizers can be produced. Methane forms the basis of a number of man-made fibres, such as Orlon, Dynel and Acrilan. Thus, a single raw material, petroleum, can be converted into a wide range of finished products. The problem facing the planners was one of testing whether a petroleum-based complex would be economically viable if located in Puerto Rico.

It was felt that the most promising type of petroleum-based complex would be one which produced petro-fuel oil, fertilizers and synthetic fibres. The fertilizer could be used locally or exported to the south eastern United States market. The synthetic fibre could be used in the manufacture of textiles, using the local unskilled labour force. Certain components of some petro-complexes could be rejected at an early stage. Antifreeze production was dismissed due to minimal local demand. Similarly, after an examination of local market conditions, the production of synthetic rubber was rejected.

The first step in the analysis for the selection of viable complex components consisted of constructing a flows table for the various activities which might fit into the complex. A condensed table for the Puerto Rican study is presented in Table 3. *The distinctions between the industrial complex and input-output tables should be noted.* The former concentrates on very finely divided sectors, or activities, which are listed across the top of the table. For example, a number of petroleum refinery prototypes are listed, each capable of producing varying amounts of certain products. Likewise, alternative conversion processes are included with the list of activities. Various products are listed down the left hand side of the table, each measured in physical terms as noted.

Table 3 Annual inputs and outputs for selected oil refinery, petrochemical and synthetic fibre activities

	Oil Refinery, Prototype 1 (1)	Oil Refinery, Prototype 4 (4)	Ethylene Separation Prototype 4 (10)	Ethylene Glycol (oxidation) (22)	Ammonia from Hydrogen (31)	Ammonia from Methane (32)	Ammonia from Ethylene (33)	Ammonia from Ethane (34)	Nitric Acid from Ammonia (43)	Dimethyl Terephthalate (air oxidation) (44)	Dacron Polymer (46)	Dacron Staple (47)	Ammonium Nitrate from Ammonia (55)	Urea from Ammonia (56)	Nylon Filament (73)
1. Crude Oil MM bbl.	−9.428	−9.428													
2. Gasoline, straight-run MM bbl.	+2.074	+1.300													
3. Gasoline, cracked MM bbl.	+1.484	+2.226													
4. Gasoline, reformed MM bbl.		+1.486													
5. Gasoline, polymerized MM bbl.	+0.219	+0.415	+0.029												
6. Naphtha, MM bbl.	+0.660	+0.707													
7. Kerosene, MM bbl.	+0.943	+0.896													
8. Diesel oil MM bbl.	+1.414														
9. Gas oil MM bbl.															
10. Cycle oil MM bbl.	+1.320	+1.980													
11. Heavy residual MM bbl.	+0.943	+4.033	+0.508												
12. Coke and carbon 10XMM lb.	+6.860	+15.050													
13. L.P.G. 10XMM lb.	+0.950	+8.900													
14. Hydrogen MM lb.	+12.780	+34.860			−2.000										
15. Methane MM lb.						−5.500									
16. Ethylene (mixed) MM lb.	+6.510	+17.410	−16.100				−6.290								
17. Ethane (mixed) MM lb.	+9.930	+32.250	−30.190					−5.780							
18. Propylene MM lb.	+3.630	+7.580	−7.580												
19. Propane MM lb.	+2.150	+5.080	−5.080												
20. Butylenes MM lb.															
21. Butanes MM lb.															
22. Pure ethylene MM lb.			+16.100	−8.300											
23. Pure ethane MM lb.			+30.190												
24. Steam MMM lb.	−0.801	−1.402	−0.148	−0.103		−0.023	−0.023	−0.023	−1.200	−0.030	−0.060	−0.500	−0.007	−0.028	−0.555
25. Power MM kw. hr.	−2.511	−3.999	−0.194	−0.800	−4.640	−5.600	−5.600	−5.600		−5.200	−2.500	−12.000	−0.170	−0.340	−16.000
26. Fuel 10XMMM Btu.	−139.000	−242.000	−2.010	−2.010		−0.450	−0.450	−0.450		−2.800	−1.000			−2.250	
34. Nitrogen MM lb.				+68.000											−2.200
35. Ethylene Glycol MM lb.				+10.000							−3.230				
39. Ammonia MM lb.					+10.000	+10.000	+10.000	+10.000	−2.860				−2.380	−5.800	
40. HCN MM lb.															
41. Acrylonitrile MM lb.															
42. Methanol MM lb.										−4.000	+3.350				
43. Sulphur MM lb.															
44. Sulphuric acid MM lb.															
45. Nitric acid MM lb.									+10.000				−7.630		
46. Paraxylene MM lb.										−6.800					
47. Dimethyl terephthalate MM lb.										+10.000	−10.100				
48. Dacron polymer MM lb.											+10.000	−10.000			
49. Dacron Staple MM lb.												+10.000			
59. Ammonium nitrate MM lb.													+10.000		
60. Urea MM lb.														+10.000	
61. Carbon dioxide MM lb.														−7.500	
74. Nylon salt MM lb.															−10.000
76. Nylon filament MM lb.															+10.000

The numerical values in the table, based on engineering data, are denoted by either a 'plus' or 'minus' sign; the plus indicating an output, while the minus denotes an input. It can be seen that Oil Refinery Prototype 1, given in column 1, requires inputs of 9.428 million barrels of crude oil, 801 million pounds of steam, 2.511 million kilowatt hours of electricity and other inputs to produce 2.074 million barrels of straight-run gasoline, 0.660 million barrels of naphtha, 1.320 million barrels of cycle oil, and other products. Similarly, the information for activity 47 (see top of Table 3) indicates the quantities of Dacron staple that can be produced from Dacron polymer, steam and electricity.

As in planning any industrial complex, a key problem in the Puerto Rican case was the selection of feasible programmes. In the analysis, a programme was defined as a set of activities that would support one another. As the determination of technical feasibility preceded the test for economic feasibility, an examination of the linkages involved was obviously crucial. Let us take a closer look at the technical linkages in one of these programmes, denoted in the study as the 'Dacron A Programme'. This particular programme employed Oil Refinery Prototype 4, which produced three sets of products. The cracking process resulted in such conventional products as gasoline, kerosene and diesel oil. Additionally, however, certain useful gases, such as hydrogen, methane, ethylene and ethane, were produced. Each of these gases could be used for the production of fertilizer. Likewise, the refinery-produced ethylene could be further processed to obtain Dacron polymer, and eventually Dacron staple which could be used for the production of textiles. The flow of products involved in this particular programme is shown in Figure 1.

Figure 1   Dacron A Programme

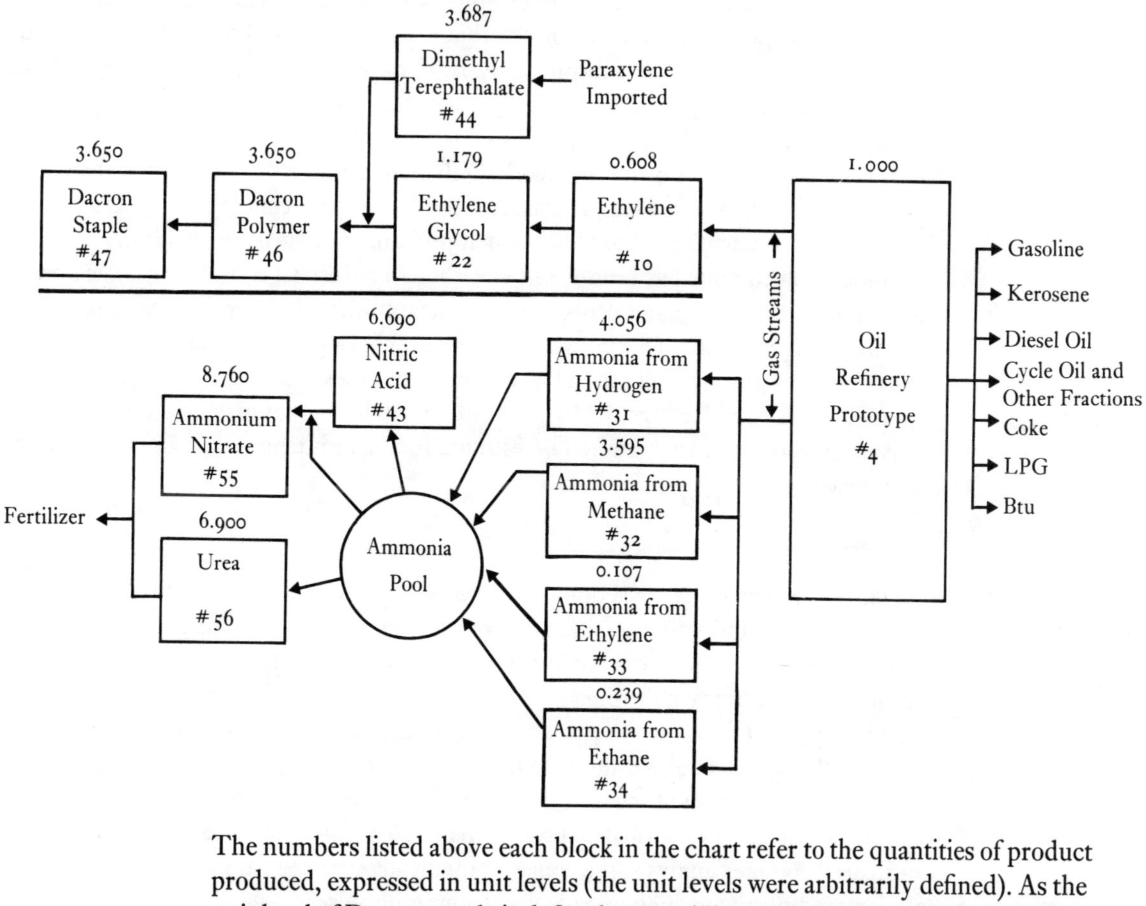

The numbers listed above each block in the chart refer to the quantities of product produced, expressed in unit levels (the unit levels were arbitrarily defined). As the unit level of Dacron staple is defined as 10 million pounds per year (from Table 3), and since 3.650 unit levels are produced, it is apparent that this programme produces 36.5 million pounds of Dacron staple. The required input level of Petroleum Refinery Prototype 4 to support this and other processes is 1.000 unit level multiplied by the quantity per unit level, 9.428 million barrels of crude petroleum. Operations at this level also produce 8.760 unit levels of ammonium nitrate (where 1 unit level is 10 million pounds) and 6.900 unit levels of urea (where 1 unit level is 10 million pounds). In this manner, the various process linkages can be made internally consistent.

The necessary inputs of capital and labour are computed separately in the industrial complex analysis. As you know, the assumptions of input-output analysis demand a proportional increase in inputs to obtain an incremental increase in output. In the case of labour and capital inputs, such an assumption is tenuous, as in reality, output might very well be increased by some degree without increasing labour and capital inputs. The industrial complex model recognises the lack of realism embodied in this assumption and allows input requirements to be computed as side calculations.

Once the technical feasibility of a potential complex is determined, the problem of economic feasibility must be confronted. In the Isardian analysis, this is tested by the comparative cost technique. The costs of producing a given quantity of various outputs is compared with the costs of producing similar outputs at competing locations. Due to the lack of resident engineers in Puerto Rico, for example, higher wage rates would be required to attract this form of skilled labour to that location, compared with some competing location in the southern United States. Textile labour, on the other hand, might be considerably less expensive. Transport costs would be expected to vary for the competing production locations and this would also have to be taken into account. Although technical linkages are an important ingredient of a successful complex, its economic feasibility determines whether or not it will survive.

Although industrial complex analysis does appear to have significant advantages over input-output analysis as a method of examining the linkages that constitute an economic complex, the method is not without its limitations (Todd, 1974), which are, in the main, shared by input-output analysis. For a start, the industrial complex model is static (that is, the model does not itself generate changes in, say, the original product mix), while what is really required is a model which is capable of generating changes from within its own framework. Only then can we adequately describe what is, after all, a dynamic growth process. A second limitation concerns its practicality; the data requirements are immense, which probably accounts for the limited number of times the technique has been applied. Although industrial complex analysis does give at least rough estimates concerning the magnitude of localization economies; urbanization economies (Sections 2.2.1 and 2.2.2) have proven more elusive. Finally, the analysis of linkages suggests a basic element of inflexibility. Either a complete multi-process complex is created at one time, a condition that may preclude the private entrepreneur with limited investment funds, or integrated production cannot take place.

4 Spatial spread of economic impulses
4.1 Introduction

As you have seen, there are serious problems associated with the use of either input-output or industrial complex analysis as methods of analysing growth in geographical space. Whereas the former technique involves levels of aggregation that frequently tend to mask the linkages that occur, the latter lacks the degree of flexibility that is required for expansion at a later date. In this section, we turn to other ways of viewing the spread of economic growth, not only among sectors, but over space as well. Although certain of the techniques presented here are perhaps less well developed, at least in a formalized sense, than either input-output analysis or industrial complex analysis, the concepts involved serve as a valuable aid to understanding the spatial spread of economic impulses.

4.2 Interfirm linkages as a mechanism for spread

One definition of economic complexes might be that they are comprised of firms that are linked together in some manner. As we have seen when examining localization economies, firms might group together to share an expert pool of skilled labour, or because transport costs of raw materials or finished goods might be minimized at some point. Florence (1961) suggests other causes for the localization of industry that may be even more important than those already considered. These factors included the possibility of division of labour among plants in a linked, or continuous process. Such linkage might also result in the location of specialist service-type firms within the complex. Although such firms may have an inadequate demand for their services if they locate near only one of their customers, the existence of a number of such customers in spatial proximity, within a complex perhaps, might lead to full utilization of a specialist firm. Two examples from areas with dynamic local economies can be used to illustrate the point.

In a pioneering study of industrial linkages, Florence (1948) found that metal industries were highly concentrated in the Midland conurbation, consisting of Birmingham and surrounding counties. These included both single process industries; such as founding, forging, galvanizing, tinning, japanning, enamelling, stamping and piercing, and component producers; such as iron and steel tube manufacturers, producers of nuts, bolts and engineering tools. As a result, other firms which used these components, such as the manufacturers of cars, jewellery, plate, stoves and pins were attracted to the complex. According to Florence, this accounted for the presence of the jewellery quarter of Birmingham, where on one short street, there were forty businesses. Twenty-five of these were in the jewellery trade itself, while ten were working for it as gem stone merchants, bullion dealers and other related enterprises. When work at any one firm exceeded that unit's capacity, work was allocated to other firms in the complex. Similarly, specific processes of the production process were carried out by different firms in the complex, each being linked by an internal transport system that resembled one that might link departments of a single large enterprise.

A number of other examples of the concentration of metal-working firms were found by Florence in the Birmingham conurbation. In West Bromwich, a location quotient (Section 2.2.1) of 40.8 was computed for the hollow-ware industry, while in Wolverhampton, the lock industry quotient was 50.9. In the small town of Dudley, which at the time of the survey had a population of only 50,000, the location quotient for the chain and anchor industry was 83.8, despite the fact that Dudley had minimal deposits of coal and iron and was far from the sea.

The Birmingham metal-processing complex can only partly be explained by the presence of a large and concentrated population. The trend toward increasing flexibility in transport over the past century, highlighted by the development of the railways and motorized transport, has probably reinforced the trend toward complexes in that they both reduce transport costs and increase the likelihood of personal contacts. Furthermore, complex formation leads to lower production costs for the generally small firms in the Birmingham area in much the same way that economies of scale cut production costs for larger firms.

In a more recent survey of industrial linkages, Keeble (1969) has examined the situation in north-west London. Of particular interest in the survey are findings with respect to three industrial groupings: metal fabricating and mechanical engineering, vehicles, and electrical engineering. Over half of the firms in these local engineering industries were linked with other neighbouring firms. Whereas most industrial firms in the north-west London area that reported their linkages with other firms were primarily of the interindustry variety, such as the provision of cardboard boxes and tin cans for food processing firms; among the 'engineering' firms, these flows were of the intra-industry types; that is, linkages with other engineering firms. Examples cited by Keeble (1969, p 172) include 'the lateral linkages of aircraft component and sub-assembly firms with local aircraft manufacturing, the diagonal linkage of standard electrical component specialists with firms assembling electrical water heaters and refrigeration equipment, and the vertical linkage of many smaller sub-contract precision engineering firms with larger mechanical engineering plants'.

It is interesting to note that a number of the engineering firms with high levels of linkages are involved primarily with executing sub-contractual orders from large firms. As Keeble notes, sub-contracting requires close co-operation and contact between the supplier and the purchaser, as the sub-contracted components must conform strictly to the purchaser's specifications as well as his production schedule. Whereas the purchaser may be content to obtain standard components, such as nuts, bolts and pipes from a distant supplier, for precision components, a nearby sub-contractor plays a vital role. As sub-contract orders are relatively easy to obtain, many smaller firms begin industrial operations in this manner, eventually graduating to the production of their own end-products.

The Keeble study also notes the fact that linkages extend to surrounding areas, implying that the dynamic nature of economic growth in north-west London may well be providing a stimulus to more distant areas. In particular, the linkages of metal finishing firms were found to extend over distances of 80 to 95 kilometres from the plant location. Figure 2 shows the spatial distribution of linkages among engineering

Figure 2   Spatial orientation of branch factory linkages in south-east England
From D. E. Keeble, 'Local industrial linkage and manufacturing growth in outer London'
Town Planning Review, 40:2 (1969), p 183

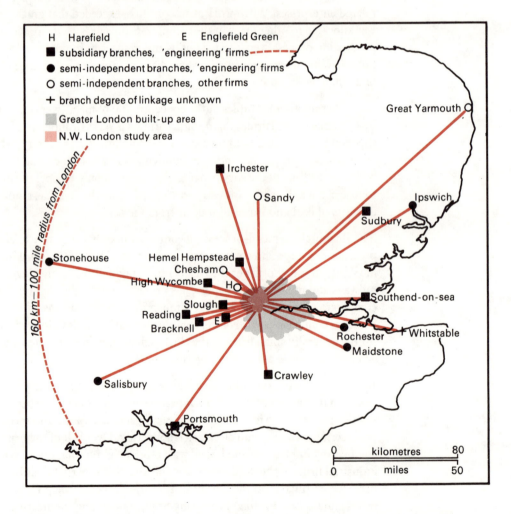

firms, with a 160-kilometre radius line apparently serving as a distance constraint. These linkages over distance are, at least partly, explained by the migration of customer firms from north-west London to more outlying locations, particularly to the new towns around London. Although the firms moved, the industrial linkages were maintained.

4.2.2 *Linkage analysis in planning complexes*

In order to apply the empirical observations on intersectoral and interregional linkages to the process of planning and analysing economic complexes, the various types of dependencies that exist among individual firms must be established. Wood (1969) has attempted to classify the types of *spatial* linkages that can exist into a four-fold typology.

1 *Process links*, defined as the movement of commodities among plants in a manufacturing process, including sub-contracting.

2 *Servicing links*, defined as the provision of equipment and maintenance services by firms external to the production unit.

3 *Marketing links*, defined as the interdependence of firms for product distribution, including wholesaling and transportation services.

4 *Financial links*, defined as ties with financial and business advisory services.

It should be apparent that the Wood classification encompasses both potential linkages between firms within the same area and between firms in different areas. By simple extension, linkages between departments within a firm could be included. The core of the production chain, regardless of the industrial organization considered, is included within the definition of the process link. As such production units are likely to be classified in the same industrial sector, it is apparent that the result of such linkages may well be the exploitation of localization economies (see Section 2.2.1).

Let us begin with a brief examination of linkages within a single firm. The modern large enterprise might well consist of a number of operations, to some degree independently managed, yet under the overall managerial umbrella of a control board of directors. Haig (1926, p 416) has described the firm as a 'packet of functions', a point later taken up by Keeble (1971), who notes that various functions can be carried out at different locations. Keeble asserts that the four activities of the firm which might most logically be carried out at different locations are: the manufacture of end-products, the manufacture of components, sales and distribution, and research and development. Smaller firms, of course, may be unable to separate these functions spatially. Yet, in large firms, interdepartmental linkages may play an analogous role to interindustry or intersectoral linkages in a complex of industries.

Moore (1972, p 259) has identified three patterns which frequently emerge in detailed analysis of this type of interfirm relationship, patterns that would be lost in the necessary aggregation for an input-output table. (See Section 3.2.) First, there is

Figure 3   Simple types of interfirm linkages

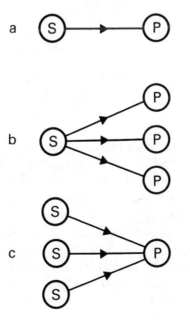

the simple interplant linkage between a supplier industry S and a purchasing industry P (Figure 3a). The second type of linkage consists of a supplier who provides inputs to several different purchasing firms (Figure 3b), a situation illustrated by the lumber industry which provides a basic input to a number of processors, who in turn produce various end-products. The third linkage type is of a firm which uses the output of a number of suppliers (Figure 3c). An example of this latter type of linkage might be characterized by the transportation vehicle sector, where a car assembly plant might use components from hundreds of other firms.

This pattern of linkages becomes increasingly complex as other firms are added to the supply network. In this instance, combinations of the three major types of industrial linkages occur, as do chain linkages among firms, where each unit further refines or processes a raw material or semi-finished product before passing it on to another firm for further processing or finishing.

The remaining three types of spatial linkages– servicing, marketing and financial– are those that might be expected to result in urbanization economies, where firms from different economic sectors, due to their proximity to the same basic resources, contribute to lower unit costs of production.

4.2.3 *Process analysis and complexes* The analysis of the relationships which go to make up an industrial process (and this might very well incorporate both intra- and interindustrial linkages), may in many cases form the necessary analytical tool for both the study and planning of economic complexes. Once these relationships are clearly set out, corporate, as well as governmental planners, are in a position to determine which additional processes might be fused onto the framework. The device also helps determine additional input needs that may be required for expansion of output. Although less precise than industrial complex analysis, the flexibility that results from process analysis may well be its foremost advantage.

Figure 4   Process analysis

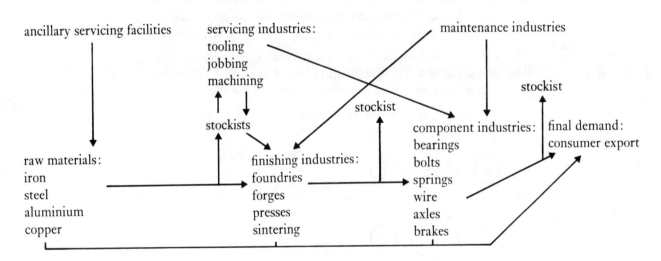

Figure 4 provides a simple illustration of the process system. This example is based on a metal-processing complex, and begins with the raw material stage, and then, through a linkage chain, progresses from the metal-finishing industries and component industries to final demand. It is evident that various servicing and maintenance industries provide inputs into the process, as stockists and as parts of the distribution trade. As Todd (1974) notes, each stage of the process is self-contained, being capable of providing products direct to final demand sources if some intracomplex link is missing. Furthermore, the system provides entrepreneurs with information on which stages of the production process offer investment possibilities. The flow diagram suggests specific locations for particular components of the complex. Such an analysis of linkages can be an important explanatory factor of why industrial growth occurs. The spatial juxtaposition of the components of the complex suggests why such growth often occurs at a point. First, however, let us examine the methods by which such growth can be transmitted.

<table>
<tr><td>

4.3 Competition for resources as a mechanism for spread

</td><td>

Economic growth can disperse from a point in space in a number of different ways. You have already seen how the linkages among firms can lead to growth both near the firm, as a complex, or some distance away, depending upon the supply and demand relationships. Additionally, however, the expansion of economic activity at a point will almost inevitably have repercussions upon economic conditions at neighbouring locations due to the spatial element in competition for resources: notably competition for land and competition for labour.

</td></tr>
<tr><td>

4.3.1 Competition for land and rent

</td><td>

In Section 2.1.2 of Unit 7, you learned that in an urban area, the utility of a specific site in that area was largely determined by its accessibility to other areas. Utility and accessibility were used as the basis for determining the spatial bid rent curve for a given activity within the urban area. You will recall that in its idealized form, this urban rent surface resembled an inverted cone, centred over the town centre.

The spread of economic activity from one point within the urban area to another might very well be affected by the urban rent surface. A number of firms, each offering similar products, might feel that they should have a town centre location. The number of sites at that point, however, are obviously limited. The firms which offer the highest rents for the available sites will obtain them, while the unsuccessful bidders will be dispersed to other parts of the area, perhaps in the periphery, an area which would be characterized by lower rent levels. Production in these periphery areas would result in economic growth there, and might also lead to the establishment of supplier firms in spatial proximity, i.e., complexes.

The urban rent surface can also affect the spatial spread of economic activity in another fashion. A productive unit which is located near the town centre, and hence at the peak of the urban rent surface, may be dependent upon suppliers who are located near the edge of the city, in areas with lower rent. These suppliers may well prefer a location close to the centrally-located firm, but may be either unable, or unwilling, to pay the rents demanded at such a location. Nevertheless, if the centrally-located firm should experience a period of growth, through the linkage mechanisms, the supplier firms will also be expected to experience growth. This growth at the edge of the city may result in the establishment of further firms to supply the supplier, with the possibility that as the production process is extended at that location, a further complex may develop at the periphery of the urban area.

It is entirely possible that a new firm may locate in the complex which replaces, or partially replaces, the role played by the centrally-located firm. On the other hand, the rationalization of the production process may take place by the centrally-located firm transferring its own operations to the complex.

Yet one must never forget the potentially fluid nature of the urban rent surface. As firms are attracted to the periphery, the rent surface at that point is likely to be raised, distorting the originally conical shape. What had once been a low rent area might very well be transformed into an area characterized by rising rents which could some day, depending on the degree of development that actually takes place, rival the town centre as the summit on the rent gradient surface. If this did indeed occur, the growth might once more be transferred to still another location, one with lower rents, and the entire process might be repeated.

</td></tr>
<tr><td>

4.3.2 Competition for labour

</td><td>

A further resource that may be in short supply in an area experiencing rapid economic growth is labour. As we know, industrial activity, particularly in the nineteenth century, was concentrated at the centre of the city largely because of the proximity

</td></tr>
</table>

to labour supplies. If the economic activity in a particular city was of a dynamic nature, with continually increasing demand for the services of labour, the wage rates of labour would be expected to rise. A part of the increasing demand for labour would be met by in-migration from other areas, while the remainder of the available jobs would only be filled by bidding labour away from other firms by offering higher wages.

For the firm, when faced with increasing costs of labour services, there would be the temptation to migrate from a city centre location. Nevertheless, given the dynamic nature of the urban economy, as well as the established linkages between the firm, its suppliers and its customers, a move no further than to the edge of the city might be contemplated. The advantage of such a move, in addition to maintaining technical relationships, is that the trained labour force would still be near at hand, and probably at a lower wage rate if accessibility is increased among those workers who live some distance from the city centre.

As a result of the competition for resources, particularly land and labour, not only would the city be expected to grow economically, but also to spread out physically. Improvements in the urban transport system would be expected to reinforce this outward trend, as such improvements increase the accessibility of outlying sites. Among American cities, the westward expansion of Chicago, the spread of Boston to both the north and south, as well as the creation of peripheral cities around the borders of Los Angeles, with the resulting urban sprawl of the latter city, seem to be illustrations of this competition for resources. Although obviously the use of the term 'wave-like spread' is an over-simplification, given the hops and jumps that are contained in such movement, this description seems to fit the pattern that has been established in many cities of the world.

4.4 Diffusion

An alternative way of looking at the spread of economic activity from a single point through a spatial hinterland is by means of the diffusion model (you may have already encountered diffusion models in the course 'New Trends in Geography', D281, Unit 16). As Hägerstrand (1965, p 27) notes, the spread of cultural areas in Europe has traditionally been studied by means of a series of maps, each for a succeeding time period, showing the spatial distribution, or diffusion, of cultural elements at that specific time. Although this tool of geographical analysis has been used primarily for studies of migration and the spread of innovations and cultural traits, Zelinsky (1962) has observed that such a framework could readily be applied to the decentralization of industry, and hence, to the transmission of economic impulses.

According to Brown (1968, p 9), the typical situation in spatial diffusion contains six basic elements:

1 an area of environment;

2 time which may be divided into successive intervals, designated as t, $t + 1$, $t + 2$, etc.;

3 an item being diffused in the environment over time;

4 nodes of origination; places where the item is located at time t;

5 nodes of destination; places where the item is located for the first time in time $t + 1$; and

6 paths of movement between nodes of origin and destination.

The probability that some trait will be transferred between two points during a given time depends to some degree upon the characteristics of the nodes of origin and destination. In considering the diffusion of economic innovation and development, it is apparent that rapidly growing firms which employ modern techniques are more likely to have a spatial influence on *nodes of destination* than firms which are small and content with archaic technology. The most important determinant of spatial spread, however, is linked to the relationship that might exist between place of origin and destination.

One of the more important of these factors that affects diffusion between two places, and one you have encountered in a number of other contexts (e.g. Units 3, 8, 9), is the effect of distance between the two nodes, or the *distance decay function*. Diffusion can occur in two distinct forms, either in the form of waves from a central point, or as a jump from one point to some distant point, with the trait then diffusing from that new location. In the industrial context, both forms of diffusion lead to changes in the structure of the economic activity surface, building it up at one location, spreading it out at another. In either form, the effect of distance might be a crucial variable, as it influences the level of communication that exists between the points. An entrepreneur searching for a location for a new branch plant, is probably more familiar with potential sites close to his present location than sites far away. Similarly, as you have seen, seller and purchaser relationships, another factor which can result in the spatial spread of demand, are more likely to be among firms that are near one another than widely spread apart. Once again, our familiar friend, the distance decay function, seems applicable.

Another factor that can affect the spread of economic impulses within the diffusion framework is the *acquaintance relationship* between the nodes of origination and nodes of destination. To a degree, this type of linkage is also affected by the distance separating the nodes. An industrialist searching for a new source of supply might well prefer to deal with someone he has had business with in the past than someone else that he does not know. Although the number of acquaintances would be expected to decline with distance, in an age of modern communication and business conventions, distant acquaintances are not only a possibility, but may be the basis for the formation of an economic linkage.

A third factor that could affect spatial diffusion is the existence of *intervening opportunities* between nodes. As in the case of trade flows (Section 3.3, Unit 3), nearer markets or sources of supply might be linked to the original node before further nodes are exploited. As with the case of the circle of acquaintances, intervening opportunities are closely linked to the effect of distance.

It is evident that distance from the node of origination plays a key role in diffusion theory. An example of how such principles might be made operational will further illustrate the importance of the distance factor. Hägerstrand (1965) employs a simple diffusion model to study the spatial spread of innovation. Although the example deals with the spread of innovation, there is no reason to believe that the spread of economic impulses should not behave in a similar manner. Hägerstrand assumes that population is evenly distributed over a plane and that an innovator lives in the centre of the plane. For the sake of simplicity, this population can be grouped in grid squares. The rules for the diffusion process used in this model include:

1   that the innovation is adopted as soon as someone else hears of it;

2   that information is spread exclusively through private conversations at pairwise meetings;

3   that the conversations take place at constant intervals of time; and

4   the choice of receiver of the information is determined on a random basis by empirically-determined probabilities.

If the Hägerstrand grid contains five squares from left to right and five from top to bottom, a table of probabilities can be constructed, indicating the likelihood of the innovator in the middle square telling someone else in any of the squares of his invention. This table, as shown in Table 4a, would have 25 cells.

Table 4 Hägerstrand's probability table

a. The base table

b.   A probability table used to study linkages in an area of Sweden

P_1	P_2	P_3	P_4	P_5
P_6	P_7	P_8	P_9	P_{10}
P_{11}	P_{12}	P_{13}	P_{14}	P_{15}
P_{16}	P_{17}	P_{18}	P_{19}	P_{20}
P_{21}	P_{22}	P_{23}	P_{24}	P_{25}

0.0096	0.0140	0.0168	0.0140	0.0096
0.0140	0.0301	0.0547	0.0301	0.0140
0.0168	0.0547	0.4431	0.0547	0.0168
0.0140	0.0301	0.0547	0.0301	0.0140
0.0096	0.0140	0.0168	0.0140	0.0096

If the distance decay funtion was assumed to operate symmetrically in all directions outward from the centre of the grid, the highest probability value would refer to other persons in the innovator's own grid square, square 13. This grid constitutes a *probability surface* with a central peak, as shown in Table 4b. These probabilities would decline in all directions, and their sum would, of course, add to unity. In time period t + 1, the innovator would tell someone of his invention. This person would most likely be located in the central grid square, that one with the highest probability value. If, however, the node of destination were not in the central grid, then the next most likely possibilities would be in those with the probability value 0.0547 (grid squares 8, 12, 14 or 18 in Table 4a), while the third most likely set would have the probability value 0.0301 (squares 7, 9, 17 and 19). In period t + 2, the innovator would have another conversation, as would the recipient of the message in period t + 1. The probability table shown in Table 4b would be relevant for the innovator in period t + 2, and would be adjusted to centre over the receiver of the t + 1 message to determine who the two recipients of the period t + 2 message would be. In period t + 3, there would be four nodes of origination, while in t + 4, there would be eight. The most likely pattern of diffusion would be a wave-like pattern emanating from the central grid square, given the assumptions and probability values of the example. This pattern could, if the probability values were changed, be shifted to a jump pattern if the analyst felt that this best reflected reality.

An examination of the spread of economic activity in a number of countries suggests that it could be described by a suitably calibrated diffusion model. The best example is probably the westward development of the United States. Beginning with a modest enclave of manufacturing activity in the eighteenth century, centred in the Boston-New York area, a definite spread occurred throughout the nineteenth century. Although the predominant route was slowly across New York, Pennsylvania, Ohio, Michigan toward Chicago, there were various jumps, stimulated by mining and transportation activities in California. The initial pattern was of two predominant areas of economic activity: the north-east manufacturing belt, extending from New England to the Upper Midwest Region and California. At later dates, activity increased in Texas (Dallas, Fort Worth, Houston), in the south (particularly around Birmingham), the north-west (Seattle, Tacoma, Portland) and the Midwest (Kansas City, Omaha, St. Louis). As economic activity diffused from one location to another in the United States, the industrial activity surfaces were built up at various points, and then spread from those points into the hinterlands of the various urban areas.

Pred (1971) has suggested a hierarchical model of diffusion that incorporates many of the relevant elements of this process. He hypothesises (in terms of diffusion of messages) that the nodes of origination were comprised of the highest order places within the urban hierarchy. The messages were then transmitted progressively through the lower order urban areas. Returning to the United States it should be apparent that as the industrial activity surfaces were raised with westward movement of economic development, lower order cities would increase in importance, transmitting activity to other still lower order places within their own hinterland. In this manner, both the jump pattern of diffusion, as well as the wave patterns, could be incorporated to describe the industrial development of the United States.

5 Growth pole theory as a synthesis of agglomeration and transmission

To this point, we have examined the importance of various types of linkages between productive units, and the resulting potential for agglomeration, as a method of transmitting economic impulses from one industrial sector to another. We have also seen how the diffusion process can be used to describe and predict the spatial spread of economic growth. As you have seen, both linkages and diffusion can lead to shifts in the surfaces which determine the levels of economic activity at any given location. At this stage, these diverse elements of theory can be integrated by use of the concept of the growth, or development pole.

5.1 The concept of growth poles

Many of the initial ideas concerning growth poles were developed by the French economist, François Perroux, who observed that 'growth does not appear everywhere and all at once; it appears in points or development poles, with variable intensities, it spreads along diverse channels and with varying terminal effects for the whole of the economy'. (Perroux, 1964, p 143).

In Perroux's original work on the pole concept, it is apparent that he considered it to be a non-spatial concept. In fact, to Perroux the growth pole was an abstract economic concept, referring to the propulsive linkages that might be established among economic enterprises. He defined the concept as a 'centre (poles or foci) from which centrifugal forces emanate and to which centripetal forces are attracted. Each centre being a centre of attraction and repulsion has its proper field which is set in the field of all other centres' (1950, p 27). Within this broad definition, as Darwent (1969, p 6) has observed, the Perrouxian 'poles are therefore best regarded simply as sectors of an economy represented by an input-output matrix in which the growth effects can be transmitted across the rows and columns'.

The concept of growth poles as relating to geographical space, was developed by Boudeville (1957, p 2). Whereas Perroux viewed economic space strictly in the abstract, Boudeville contended that economic space 'is an application of economic variables on or in a geographical space, through a mathematical transformation which describes an economic process'. As a result, it is possible to view the growth pole concept in two rather distinct contexts. In the Perrouxian context, growth poles can be viewed purely in terms of economic linkages. Hence, the Renault car manufacturing firm might form a growth pole, with linkages to suppliers throughout France, but a pole which is independent of its geographical location in Paris. On the other hand, growth poles can be viewed in a geographical sense, with interlinked firms forming an economic complex at a location, with certain advantages for each component, as well as potential supply and demand advantages for new firms. This crucial distinction is one that has eluded a number of experienced regional analysts. In our analysis, we will concentrate upon the latter spatial aspects of the growth pole concept as they relate to growth and development at a given location, recognizing, of course, that the impulses produced can spread to other locations.

5.2 Prerequisites of a growth pole

To this stage, it appears that growth poles are primarily based on abstract philosophical arguments that may appear to have limited value to regional growth and development. Although the underlying theoretical structure that is necessary to fully integrate growth poles with regional growth has not been fully developed, the idea has an intuitive appeal and has rapidly become an essential ingredient of many regional plans. Despite the modest amount of empirical research into the growth pole phenomenon, certain tentative conclusions have been established which provide information on how growth poles might be expected to develop, as well as the characteristics of this development.

5.2.1 *Dominance*   Growth poles are the result of a self-sustaining economic force. This economic force can be either a firm or an urban area. As most cities are the result of economic activity, and since they grow and decline as a result of the fortunes of that activity, the firm can be seen to constitute the focal point of growth pole development. There appear to be certain characteristics of firms that result in economic growth of the regions in which they are located. The lead firm in regional development is almost always large and can be expected to employ the latest technological advances in its production process. Furthermore, the lead firm is a growing firm: through time it produces an increasing proportion of its area's product as well as a growing percentage of the nation's output in its own particular industrial sector. As the lead firm grows, its negotiating strength increases, it becomes a dominating influence to both its suppliers and its clients, and perhaps most importantly, it creates favourable conditions for the development of agglomerative economies. Regional economic growth would be expected to result from the direct and indirect linkages connecting the lead firm with other components of the regional economy.

Erickson (1974) has analysed the effect of one lead firm upon the region in which it was located, providing quantitative estimates of the linkages generated. The study focuses on the Boeing Company, located in the Puget Sound area of the U.S. Pacific North West. During the period from 1963–1968, the Boeing Company experienced a significant rise in the demand for the commercial aircraft that it produces. This rise in demand, primarily of the regional export variety (see Unit 4, Section 5.2), resulted in both growth of the company itself and economic growth of the whole area. The externally induced growth was the result of linkages connecting Boeing with its suppliers. The analysis not only provides additional evidence on the validity of export base theory, but also serves as an example of potential linkages that can lead to self-sustaining growth within a growth pole.

Erickson identifies three sets of linkages which result in induced growth as a result of the rise of the lead firm:

1 linkages within the technological system;

2 linkages within the capital goods system; and

3 linkages within the lateral-induced system.

The technological system linkages refer to those connections between the lead firm, its suppliers and its customers. These consist of two types of situations; suppliers of inputs to Boeing's production are said to be backward-linked, while the customers who purchase Boeing's output are forward-linked. Backward linkage is perhaps most easily understood by examining the transactions presented in an input-output table. As production of the lead firm increases, greater amounts of interindustry inputs are required, resulting in growth of suppliers, but also, growth in those firms that provide inputs to those suppliers. Forward-linked firms may well prosper as a result of external economies that may result from growth of the lead firm. As economies of scale are exploited by the lead firm at higher levels of production, the savings in costs may be passed onto customers. Additionally, technologically superior products may result, another bonus for the customers of the lead firm.

In contrast to the technological system which provides current inputs to the lead firm, the capital goods system provides productive equipment. As the demand for the lead firm's output rises, increasing amounts of plant and equipment may be required to expand output. Orders may be placed with the supplier of tools, presses and other equipment, as well as with construction firms which build buildings to house the expanding production process. As we shall see in the Boeing case, even where regional links to the technological system may be weak, a large proportion of the capital goods system would be expected to be regionally orientated.

The lateral-induced system might be defined as the indirect changes that occur within the economy as a result of increased economic activity in the productive process. These linkages are directly associated with the size of the economic base multipliers relevant to the area under consideration. As the lead firm expands output, resulting in increased demand for the products of backward-linked components of the technological system, as well as for the capital goods system, additional income is generated. Such income results in increased demand for the products of other enterprises in the area, whether they be in manufacturing, trade or services, as well as a rise in the services provided by local government.

During the period of Erickson's analysis, Boeing fulfilled the requirements of a lead firm in a growth pole. Shipments increased by 11 per cent annually compared with an increase of only just over 5 per cent for non-aerospace firms in Washington State. Whereas in 1963, Boeing produced 7.7 per cent of the total value of shipments from U.S. aerospace firms, by 1967 this percentage had risen to 9.5. Over the period, employment at Boeing rose from 100,400 to 142,400.

As the forward linkages in the technological system consisted primarily of aircraft shipments to airlines outside of the region, the backward linkages were found to be of greater importance in the analysis. The value of intermediate inputs into Boeing production increased by over 260 per cent between 1963 and 1967, from $521 million to $1,370 million. However, due to the weakness in regional technological linkages regional inputs rose from only $59 million to no more than $164 million. As the area's inputs rose at a faster rate than total inputs, it suggests that the firms in the area did experience significant growth. The distinction between spatial and non-spatial growth poles is apparent here. Based on technological linkages, Boeing obviously serves as a lead firm for growth poles of both types.

The impact from capital expansion was far more localized in nature than that resulting from the technological linkages. In 1966 and 1967, Boeing was expanding productive capacity for the construction of the 747 jumbo jet airliner. The capital equipment required for this as well as other ventures, consisted of productive machinery and buildings. Although much of the productive equipment was imported from other regions, the investment in buildings led to increased activities among firms lying near to Puget Sound in Washington State. The total capital investment by Boeing during the period amounted to over $590 million, of which about $300 million went to the regional construction industry. Backward linkages from the construction industry to building supply firms are frequently strong, due to the problems associated with transporting many building materials. In Washington State, it is estimated that, on the basis of multiplier analysis, these purchases from the construction industry alone generated over $850 million during the growth period.

Linkages between Boeing and the lateral-induced system would also be expected to have a significant regional impact. Increases in the lead firm's payments of wages and salaries, as well as local taxes, result in an induced rise in consumption expenditure both by households and by local government. The injection of such funds into the local income stream results in further rises in regional prosperity. Interestingly, it was discovered that in the case of Boeing's expansion, the laterally induced rises in income within the state economy declined from 1963 to 1967. Erickson speculates that this was probably due to a 'decrease in regional value created per dollar of aerospace sales, differences in structural interdependence and by the expansion of imports in the regional economy' (Erickson, 1974, p 134).

The Boeing Company, then, seems to fulfil the requirements of the lead firm in growth pole analysis. The comparison between growth poles and economic base theory is hard to avoid at this stage. The success of the growth pole is obviously dependent upon a market. In the case of manufacturing, rises in output will frequently be the result of rises in the demand for the product from outside of the region. This is particularly true in the case of large firms, such as Boeing. At the same time, however, the scale of a growth pole itself can be variable in such analysis. Any cluster of firms, interdependent upon one another, could be viewed as a growth pole even if their level of output was relatively modest. The success or failure of a growth pole is a function of the dynamic nature of the lead firm. Hence, growth poles composed of small firms, possibly supplying regional demand (in contrast to export demand), may be successful, although at a much more modest level.

A second point that is of paramount importance, particularly in the Boeing case, is that the process is reversible, in exactly the same way as Myrdal's (1963) theory of circular causation (Unit 6). The dynamic aspects of dominance in growth pole analysis by the lead firm linked to other components of the regional economy is transmitted by multipliers. As long as the lead firm continues to assert its economic strength, the regional economy, through these linkages, continues to grow. If, however, as in the case of Boeing after 1968, the lead firm enters a declining period, the multipliers work in reverse, resulting in contraction of income, employment, migration to the region and other measures of regional prosperity.

5.2.2 *Polarization*

If a lead firm is established in a region, with the expected consequences among other firms, that is, linkages of various types resulting in external economies, a growth pole or growth centre situation may result. Although this development will have advantageous results at and around the location of the pole, it will also tend to create unfavourable circumstances at other locations further away. These effects are termed polarization by Hirschman (1958) and are identical to Myrdal's 'backwash' effects (1963), as discussed in Unit 6. The magnitude of the polarization effects caused by a growth pole location are dependent upon the distance from the area affected by the pole. For the convenience of this discussion, we can divide them into the effect at or very near the pole and those effects which occur further away. As you will see, these effects also have differing impacts over time.

As the lead firm in a growth pole situation expands its production, other firms within the same area are affected. If the smaller firms provide inputs into the lead firms productive process, they too would experience a period of growth. If, however, they are not linked to the lead firm in any way, the most likely result will be an increase in their own cost of production. As the lead firm increases its employment to meet its own demand, regional wages are likely to rise. If physical expansion in productive capability is required by the lead firm, the land price surface may rise. The price of building supplies might also increase, leading to a general rise in the costs of the construction industry. This localized inflation may even affect the costs facing the trade and service sector. If unemployment in the area economy is at a low level, the price of housing might also be expected to rise, due to the in-migration of new workers, lured by the prospects of the high wages offered by the lead firm. Production units which are in no way linked to the lead firm are forced to pay higher costs for labour, the services of the construction industry and for land if they wish to expand their own plant. The localized inflation will lead to further wage demands by the workers in the non-linked plants as the cost of goods and services in the area economy rises.

The impact of these rising costs may have a profound effect upon the region's more traditional industries, particularly those which are unable to increase production due to stability of demand, those which have insufficient reserve funds to invest in modernization to achieve higher productivity and hence pay higher wages, those experiencing strong interregional or international trade competition and those in direct wage competition with the lead industry. An analysis of the shoe industry in the New England region of the United States (Choguill, 1970) revealed that when faced with all of these factors, but particularly with the higher wages offered by the lead firms in the regional growth industry, electronics, shoe firms either closed permanently, or migrated to lower wage areas in the southern United States.

The immediate effects of the success of the lead firm might appear as rises in the wage and other production cost surfaces. If the time period encompassed by the lead firm's rise is relatively long, however, other effects might be felt. Congestion might occur, hampering the transfer of unfinished and finished goods and leading to a general rise in the production cost surface. As the area's population grows, there will be an increased demand for the services of local government. The local transport network may require modernization and expansion. Other infrastructural items may be operating at or near full capacity, resulting in the requirement for new investment. In the longer period, then, the urban economy may experience dis-economies of scale, resulting in higher taxes for lower levels of urban services. Eventually the demands for decentralization of industry may be heard.

Polarization effects are also to be expected to influence places further afield (Hirschman, 1958). The success of an area's lead firm, and the growth of economic complexes that might result, are soon known throughout a nation. Investment funds which might previously have been available to producers in lesser developed areas may be transferred to the growth centre. Migration of the most able workers, managers and entrepreneurs may occur from the more stagnant areas to the growth centre and its hinterland (Units 6, 9, 10 and Okun and Richardson, 1961).

In the longer run, the effect upon these less prosperous, less accessible areas can worsen. If these areas specialize in the production of agricultural commodities and other primary products, serving as a source of supply to the growth centre, expanding demand in the latter may result in little more than inflation in the more remote areas. As the price of primary products increases, the growth centre may shift its sources of supply either to other areas within the nation or to other nations through international trade. For the depressed area, such a situation may result not only in loss of productive labour and capital, but also in the longer run, in loss of markets as well.

In the long run, there may be non-economic repercussions for these outlying areas (Myrdal, 1963). They may no longer be able to afford the social services that are essential to their growth, such as education and medical facilities, with the consequence that the population would become less educated and less healthy, factors which might limit future increases in productivity. The political balance of power might shift to the growth centre (and its satellites) resulting in a still bleaker future for those remaining in the outlying areas.

5.2.3   Spread effects   Although polarization can have a profound effect upon locations away from the growth pole, the pole does have certain beneficial effects as well. You have already learned of certain of these 'spread effects' in Unit 6 (Myrdal, 1963). Again, as in the case of polarization, these spread effects, or a 'trickling down', to employ Hirschman's term (1958), can be divided, somewhat arbitrarily, into those affecting the hinterland and those affecting outlying areas.

Hinterland spread effects in the short run may be characterized as consisting primarily of increased demand by various economic operators near the growth pole. As the result of linkages to the lead firm or the lead complex, a stimulus is transmitted (in direct, indirect or induced manners) to other firms in the area (Section 5.2.1). Employment opportunities are more abundant. In the longer run, the urban tax base may be improved, allowing for the expansion of urban services, leading to at least a delay of the time when urban dis-economies overcome the economies that might result from urban growth and the more efficient use of infrastructural investments.

Although it might be expected that spread effects on outlying areas may be relatively weak in the short run, in the longer period, a more beneficial effect may be felt. As the wealth of growth poles increases, government instituted income transfers may occur to alleviate the pronounced differentials that may be developed. As congestion occurs near the growth pole, the incentive for decentralization to lower cost production regions may take place, with migration of firms to these areas, Also, as you have seen, innovation is not tied to any single area, and may be expected to diffuse from the growth centre to lesser developed areas. Such a transfer may be expected to raise the marginal productivity of labour in these places, a factor that would generate further rises in their income.

5.2.4 Polarization and spread effects combined

As we have noted, polarization and spread effects have a variable effect over space as one moves away from a growth pole location. These effects can be summarized by use of the surface concept diagram shown in Figure 5 comparing their relative magnitudes in the short run.

From the illustration, it is apparent that spread effects are strongly influenced by the effect of distance. At locations near to the growth pole itself, it is expected that the effect of linkages will be strong, but that this effect will decline at distances further away. From what you know about diffusion processes, you would expect both the spread of economic impulses and of innovation to decline in a similar and reinforcing manner.

Conversely, particularly in the short run, one would expect the surface defined by polarization, or backwash, to demonstrate a fairly weak effect at locations near the growth pole. The magnitude of this force would be expected to rise fairly steeply, having a profound effect on locations just outside the growth pole's own hinterland and then declining as one moves further and further away.

With greater distances, the relative strengths of the two competing forces may well be influenced by circumstances outside the area. In our diagram, polarization effects are pictured as more potent than the spread effects. Depending upon the linkages that may exist between the growth pole and outlying areas, this general relationship may differ in various regions. Nevertheless, considering the arguments presented in this unit, it seems reasonable that these general relationships between the two would be expected to manifest themselves in the manner shown.

5.3 An intuitive evaluation of growth poles

As we noted at the outset of our discussion on growth poles, the idea has strong intuitive appeal. As we look about us, we see various economic complexes, growth poles if you will, which have a positive impact upon their hinterland. Furthermore, the growth pole concept conveniently wraps up many of the diverse elements of regional growth theory, such as linkages, agglomeration and diffusion. Finally, we can see the close relationship that exists between growth poles and the macro-concepts discussed in Block II.

Nevertheless, although certain theoretical elements are included in the growth pole concept, the idea still leaves many unanswered questions. A truly comprehensive theory should give us some idea of how growth is initiated and where it is likely to occur. It should provide us with information on how it will be transmitted both to other sectors within an economy and also to other areas within the nation. Finally, a dynamic theory should offer insight on how growth can be maximized over time, how governments can establish positive policies to promote spread effects, how investment resources should be distributed and how the goals of society can be met.

Although the growth pole concept does provide certain suggestive hints to the answers of these questions, it should be apparent to you that much room for theoretical advancement still remains. Perhaps the most important unanswered question is why growth occurs at a location in the first place. In classical location theory, the answer to this question is intimately related to the problem of finding a minimum cost location. Demand concepts were grafted onto this construction, but it was still discovered that certain industries were, in all probability, located neither at a

Figure 5   Spread and polarisation effects

A.   2-dimensional comparison between Spread (S-S′) and Backwash (B-B′) effects.

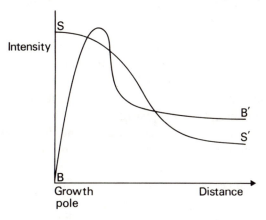

B.   Spread effect – a 3-dimensional representation

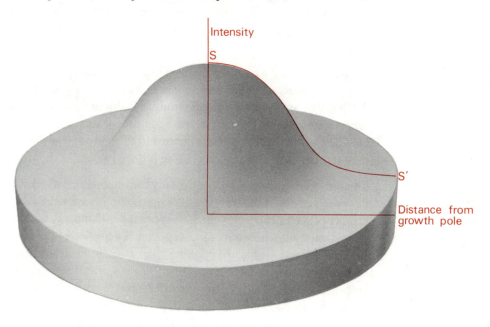

C.   Backwash effect – a 3-dimensional representation

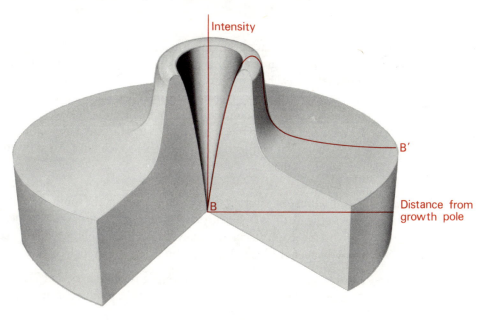

minimum cost point, nor at a maximum demand point, and yet they seemed to prosper, These 'foot-loose' industries seemed to constitute a new field of analysis for location analysts, resulting in the coining of such terms as 'satisficing', in contrast to 'maximizing' (Simon, 1957).

It is apparent how firms located at their least cost location could well become the propulsive firm in a growth pole situation. Yet, are firms such as Boeing at their least cost locations? Given the modest regional impact of the technological-linkage system (see p 80) one would probably be forced to conclude that it was not. What is missing from the growth pole concept is the explanation of how, what is probably a foot-loose firm, could survive at a non-minimum cost location, and then, at a later date, transform the surrounding area by its growth. In the Boeing case, it is apparent that technological innovations and the creation of external economies played important roles. Yet, the growth pole concept tells us little about innovation processes, and while largely based on the concept of external economies (and agglomeration) provides little information about how these develop. Although linkage theory provides much of the basis for the development of growth poles, very little linkage analysis is actually considered by the writers on the subject. The normal methods of analysing growth situations are by the use of either input-output or industrial complex models, failing to recognize the inherent problems of using static techniques to study a dynamic process.

It would seem that a more generalized linkage analysis, blended with a recognition of diffusion processes, might yield a sounder basis for analysis. Not only could flexibility be incorporated into the study, but this in turn would allow for the consideration of the dynamic aspects required for such a theory. The linkages included would necessarily incorporate intrafirm linkages (such as those which were important in the Boeing agglomeration process) as well as those among firms.

You must recognize then, in considering the importance of growth poles, that you have reached one of the frontiers of regional economic analysis. In assessing the validity of such a concept, you should remember that many of the empirical and theoretical studies necessary for acceptance or rejection of the idea have not yet been carried out. Unlike the economic base concept, which is based on rather straightforward concepts that can readily be empirically tested, the notion of growth poles as a means of transmitting growth is far more complex and difficult to test. Although various elements of growth poles have been tested, the real need is for an integrated empirical examination of the entire concept. This need is, as yet, unfulfilled. Only in the years to come will we know the true potential of the growth pole concept.

6 Case studies of the growth pole concept

To this stage, we have been concerned primarily with establishing a definitional basis for the notion of growth poles. Before closing this unit, let us direct our attention to studies that have been made of two growth poles in France. These examples further illustrate the problems involved with analysing the impact of growth. The examples encompass diverse circumstances, as one concerns the development of a natural resource in a region, while the second relates to a large non-industrial economic unit, although one with industrial ramifications, which was located by government decision in a village.

6.1 The case of Lacq

The discovery of natural gas supplies at Lacq, in the south-west of France (see the map in Figure 6), is frequently cited as a classic case of growth pole development. Bernard (1970, pp 76–79) has analysed the impact of the resulting economic activity, not only upon the immediate area, but upon the French economy as well.

In 1957, production of high-pressure, high-sulphur content gas wells at Lacq began. A complex of industries was established in the production area, including such components as purified gas producers, sulphur producers, electric power generators, aluminium processers and petrochemical works. To some, the impact of this gas production was disappointing, as practically none of the raw materials produced, such as sulphur, aluminium and chemicals, were processed locally. Similarly, most of the gas produced was transferred to industrial units in Bordeaux and Toulouse. Employment in the complex itself was relatively modest, amounting to about 7,500 workers after the construction period. Decision-making mostly took place in Paris and profits were reinvested at locations other than Lacq.

Figure 6   Lacq: location map

Nevertheless, according to Bernard, this represents only an initial approach to the total assessment of the impact on the local administrative region, the Department of Basses-Pyrenees. Information on wages paid is available for 1964. Additionally, this information can be divided into wages arising from three types of activity: direct, indirect and induced. By 1964, it would be expected that the remuneration paid to construction workers and other investment activity personnel would have been completed, and that the wage data represent a payment for operating the complex, a payment that would be expected to continue into the longer period of analysis.

The direct effect of wage payments at the complex, that is the annual amount paid to its employees, amounted to 80.66 million francs, which is nearly 11 per cent of the total wage bill for the Department. Indirect effects can be divided into two parts. The first consists of wages arising within the Department due to demand for goods and services from the complex. The second part represents demands which were filled from enterprises based outside of the Department, but were working at the site of the complex. The former were evaluated to be 16.94 million francs in 1964, while the latter were 40 million francs. Given the payments for the latter type of activity, one would expect, *a priori*, that the leakages to other areas would be significantly higher than in the case of nearby firms. This differential also suggests that the linkages between activities in the complex and its hinterland are relatively weak, at least compared with the corresponding links with other areas. This situation is comparable with the technologically-linked system in the Boeing study. Induced effects within the Departmental economy were assessed at 19.2 million francs. In evaluating the impact of a spatially-linked growth pole, this figure is of great importance and is surprisingly low. If the analyst excludes indirect effects to externally based firms from the total of all effects, the complex generates just over 15 per cent of total wages paid in the Department, while including this amount raises the figure to almost 21 per cent.

Even by using the most conservative set of figures, a frequent necessity in regional analysis, it can be seen that the Lacq complex makes a significant contribution to the Departmental economy. Certain industries in the area would, of course, be expected to benefit more than others, as linkages with the electricity generating industry, engineering industries and transport would be expected to be crucial for the activities of the complex. Perhaps most importantly, the Lacq complex illustrates the distinction between spatially linked poles (growth centres) in the Boudevillian sense and the abstract non-spatially linked poles of Perroux. The Lacq complex obviously plays both roles, inducing local activities as well as providing vital raw materials to the national industrial economy. Whether or not the complex fulfils what is perhaps the most crucial criteria of growth poles, continued generation of growth, depends upon output levels at later dates. Intuitively, one can imagine that raw material-based complexes are less likely to fill this role than one based on secondary industries. Primary material production depends foremost upon the supply of the resource, but also upon the productive capacity of the extractive industry. Reserves might represent a binding constraint in the Lacq case. On the other hand, until reserves begin to decline as a result of depletion, the short-term downward spirals that might affect manufacturing activity in periods of declining demand may be avoided in a natural resource complex. Nevertheless, in long run analysis, we need merely remember the case of the north-east of England (Section 5.3, Unit 4) to recognise the problems that can arise from a growth pole based on natural resources.

6.2   The case of Lannion   Another example that meets the criteria of a growth pole development, although one based on government intervention, is found in the north-west of France. In 1958, the French Government decided to establish a new branch of the National Telecommunication Study Centre (CNET) in the village of Lannion in Brittany (see the map in Figure 7). Lannion had only a population of 10,000 and was relatively

Figure 7   Lannion: location map

remote, with poor communications with the remainder of France. Again, Bernard (1970, pp 71–73) has analysed the impact of the move upon the economy of the village. As the circumstances seem to fulfil the basic requirements of the growth pole concept, one would expect an increase in linkages, as well as increasing prosperity in Lannion and surrounding areas.

At the time of the move, Lannion had virtually no industry. However, located in a traditional 'backwash' area that had long suffered from a lack of employment opportunity, the region had an abundant potential labour force. By 1968, the CNET establishment itself employed 800 persons, while by 1970, it had grown to 1,300 workers. Additionally, however, the Centre has become an attraction pole to firms in the electronics industry. Five firms, employing a total of 800 persons, had established themselves adjacent to CNET. The five firms all depended to a considerable extent upon assembly orders from the Posts and Telecommunications Administration (of which CNET is also a part), although only three had direct linkages with the Lannion CNET establishment. The impact of the Centre had also diffused to neighbouring communities. Engineering enterprises in the nearby villages of Morlaix and Quimper had been awarded CNET sub-contracts. Scientific research links with the university at Rennes were also established.

As a growth pole, the Lannion case is obviously on a modest scale, yet it illustrates all of the major elements that might be expected of larger poles: a growing lead firm, increasingly important linkages not only to firms at the pole itself, but also diffusion to neighbouring areas. Although Bernard does not provide information on induced effects within the local economy, you should be able to speculate on what these might include. Additionally, although no empirical information is available on the magnitude of backwash effects, you should be able to determine why they would primarily be expected to be of the hinterland variety.

7 Conclusion

In this unit we have considered the development of economic complexes and how they might modify existing economic, social and political surfaces. Economic complexes arise because of the potentials offered by the exploitation of external economies, particularly those associated with economies of scale, localization economies and urbanization economies. This tendency for firms to agglomerate at a location is dependent upon the linkages that exist among production units. As you have seen, linkages can be viewed in a number of different ways. Input-output is concerned with linkages among broad economic sectors, while industrial complex analysis can be used to examine the linkages among activities within an industry.

In analysing the growth potential of a complex, other types of linkages need to be examined as well, including linkages within the firm, linkages between firms and even linkages to firms in other areas. By the latter type of linkage, growth at one location may be transmitted to other locations, stimulating locations some distance from the original point of growth. Nevertheless, as you have seen throughout this course, distance may be a crucial variable in the diffusion of such economic impulses.

Linkages also play a vital role in the development of growth poles. As you have seen, growth poles can be defined to include two types of phenomena: non-spatial growth poles which have direct and indirect links to other industries throughout the nation, and spatial growth poles, or growth centres, which may include groups of industries at a specific point. Although both may have an impact upon a given area, the emphasis of this unit has been on the latter type. A lead firm is essential to propel the growth at a point. Such a firm must have certain characteristics, the most important of which are that it must be large and growing. If a growth pole develops, it has certain implications both for places in its immediate vicinity and for places further afield. Polarization may occur, resulting in economic orientation toward the pole, with detrimental effects for other areas. A spread effect may also take place with other areas profiting from their own linkages with the growth pole location. The magnitude of these effects depends primarily upon the size of the lead firm as well as the degree of agglomeration that results.

Agglomeration, linkages and diffusion, then are all necessary components of the growth pole concept. Although the examples we have considered have, in the main, been concerned with industrial or industrially-related enterprises, it should be apparent that this need not necessarily be the case. The tourist complexes of southern Spain or Miami or even Blackpool may have a similar growth effect upon their hinterlands. The activities of a government might be viewed in a similar manner, resulting in centres such as Washington, D.C. and Ankara, Turkey. Consequently, the growth pole concept might have growth implications that extend far beyond the industrial sector alone.

Finally, it is apparent that although growth can occur at a point on its own, generally it results from some kind of outside influence, usually the result of governmental initiative, or at a minimum, governmental encouragement. As you turn to Block 4, where the problems and potentials associated with governmental intervention are examined, you should remember the powerful role that government can exert upon regional growth. Although the Boeing success in Seattle in the 1963–8 period was based upon the sale of commercial airliners, the reason that Boeing had the necessary investment funds for these projects, as well as the expertise to carry them out, was largely due to their earlier success at winning government contracts. The decline from the 1968 peak was largely the result of not winning other government contracts. The establishment of the National Telecommunication Study Centre at Lannion was a governmental decision, as was the development of natural resources at Lacq. The role of government in these situations, and in most growth pole situations, was crucial. Growth poles are seldom spontaneous. They are normally planned, with the planning usually originating from government.

Self-assessment questions

SAQ 1 How is the location quotient affected by the industrial classification system used?

SAQ 2 What are the inherent problems involved in using the location quotient as a method of estimating localization economies?

SAQ 3 In an input–output transactions table, what is the significance of the row entries?

SAQ 4 What is final demand in input–output terminology?

SAQ 5 How can input–output analysis be used for impact analysis?

SAQ 6 Compare industrial complex analysis with input–output analysis.

SAQ 7 How is the economic feasibility of an industrial complex programme determined?

SAQ 8 Distinguish between technical and economic feasibility in industrial complex analysis.

SAQ 9 Why would you expect the input linkage of the jewellery industry in Birmingham to be more concentrated spatially than the input linkages into the car industry?

SAQ 10 Why are sub-contracting linkages most likely to arise between firms that are located near one another?

SAQ 11 In considering intrafirm linkages, which parts of the production process are most likely to be separated from other points?

SAQ 12 What is process analysis?

SAQ 13 Compare industrial complex analysis with process analysis.

SAQ 14 How could industrial linkages affect the shape of the urban rent surface?

SAQ 15 How can industrial spread be explained by diffusion analysis?

SAQ 16 Specifically, how can intervening opportunities affect the spread of economic impulses?

SAQ 17 Distinguish between the growth pole concepts of Perroux and Boudeville.

SAQ 18 Why would Boeing be considered to be the 'lead firm' in the Puget Sound region of Washington State?

SAQ 19 Distinguish between polarization effects, as the result of a growth pole development, that would be expected at or near the pole and those some distance away.

SAQ 20 Would you consider the Lacq complex to be a successful growth pole?

SAQ 21 What criticisms can you offer of the growth pole concept?

SAQ 1   If the industrial classification system is too broad, i.e. encompasses too many diverse industries, the interpretation of industrial concentration will itself be blurred, implying perhaps a general grouping of industries at a point, but with little insight into why the group is located at that point.

SAQ 2   The location quotient suggests no more than the industries that are concentrated in an area compared with the national norm. It tells nothing of the actual benefits, or savings, that is, economies of localization, that result from that concentration.

SAQ 3   The row entries provide information concerning the value of sales by the sector represented by that particular row to each other sector, including final demand, over some given time period.

SAQ 4   Final demand represents those sectors whose demands are determined exogenously, and may include households, government, exports and investment.

SAQ 5   Input-output analysis can be used to assess the economic impact of a new development in an area by determining the value of the new demands by sector for the development, and then multiplying the values by the technical coefficients of the supplying sectors. This process is repeated until, due to leakages to final demand, the value of each additional transaction approaches zero. The transactions at each iterative round are then added.

SAQ 6   The former model is primarily used for planning purposes and is based on engineering data, whereas the latter can be employed as a descriptive device as well, using empirically-derived information. Industrial complex is concerned with the linkages among activities, including alternative processes, whereas input-output emphasises links among broad sectors. Whereas input-output is based on assumptions of linearity, certain inputs of industrial complex analysis, such as capital and labour, can be allowed to vary in a non-linear manner.

SAQ 7   It is determined by comparative cost analysis, that is, by comparing the costs of producing a given quantity of output at the site of the proposed complex with that cost at competing sites.

SAQ 8   Although an economic complex may be technically feasible, that is, the technical inputs produce the desired quantity of an output, it may not be economically feasible, meaning that it may be at an uneconomic point of production. Industrial complex analysis uses an activity matrix and product programmes to determine technical feasibility, but uses comparative cost analysis to determine economic feasibility.

SAQ 9   The car industry uses an enormous number of inputs, each of which might be produced at some minimum cost location for that component. The number of inputs into the jewellery trade, on the other hand, are relatively modest in number, and the smaller firms which characterize the industry, may produce many of the components themselves.

SAQ 10 Sub-contracting requires close co-operation and contact between the supplier and the purchaser, as the sub-contracted components must conform strictly to the purchaser's specifications as well as his production schedule.

SAQ 11 End-product manufacture, component manufacture, sales and distribution and research and development.

SAQ 12 Process analysis can be used to reveal the linkage flows that can exist between various components of an economic complex. Although much more general than input-output, the flexibility encompassed allows for planning of development of the complex over time.

SAQ 13   Although both techniques may be used in the planning of economic complexes, process analysis is far less rigid in nature than industrial complex analysis. Whereas the latter analyses in detail the flow relationships between products and various alternative activities, the former gives merely a generalized account of product flow through the productive system. Although industrial complex analysis explicitly deals with economic feasibility, in the form of process analysis that we have examined, this feasibility is not tested.

SAQ 14   If a high number of interfirm linkages is thought of as suggesting the existence of an economic complex, then growth by the complex will attract other industries which must bid for the limited number of urban sites available, probably bidding up the land rent at that location, hence distorting the surface.

SAQ 15   Successful industries generate innovation and frequently produce spin-off firms. In seeking a new location, these firms are constrained by the same limitations that affect any diffusion flow: the distance between nodes, acquaintance relationships and intervening opportunities. The spread of innovation from firms is similarly affected.

SAQ 16   An economic impulse from a node of origination will tend to move to that node of destination which is both receptive and nearest to it. A similar node of destination further away would therefore be unlikely to initially receive the impulse in the first period of time, but may receive it later.

SAQ 17   The Perrouxian growth poles were defined in the aspatial sense, as linkages among industries regardless of their location. In the Boudeville analysis, the poles exist at a specific geographical location, with linkages among industries at that location.

SAQ 18   Boeing, in the period 1963–1968 was a large firm in a high technology industry. Its production was increasing both relative to the area and within its industrial sector nationally. Furthermore, its growth had a significant impact, through linkages, on the rest of the area's economy, particularly through its capital investment and through the resulting induced effects.

SAQ 19   Within the area near the growth pole, localized inflation may result in the short run, with increases in wages paid to labour, housing and the cost of certain goods and services. In the longer period, urban diseconomies of scale may arise, largely due to congestion and the full capacity use of infrastructural investments. Further afield, investment funds and the most productive employees might migrate to the growth centre. In the longer period, the markets of the lagging areas may undergo significant change, the level of social services may suffer and the balance of political power may shift to the pole.

SAQ 20   Your conclusion depends upon the concept of growth pole that you employ. Although it had perhaps limited impact locally (in the Boudeville sense), although far from insignificant, it did affect the linkages to other sectors of the national economy (in the Perrouxian sense), providing fuel and other industrial products.

SAQ 21   Much of the necessary basis for a comprehensive and integrated theory of growth poles has not yet been developed. The idea tells us little about why growth takes place at a particular location in the first place.

References BERNARD, P. (1970) *Growth poles and growth centres in regional development. Vol III : Growth poles and growth centres as instruments of regional development and modernization with special reference to Bulgaria and France*, Geneva, United Nations Research Institute for Social Development.

BOUDEVILLE, J. R. (1957) *Problems of regional economic planning*, Edinburgh, University Press.

BROWN, L. A. (1968) *Diffusion processes and location*, Philadelphia, Regional Science Research Institute.

CHOGUILL, C. L. (1970) 'Does the shoe still fit New England' *New England economic indicators*, Federal Reserve Bank of Boston, March, pp 2–9.

DARWENT, D. F. (1969) 'Growth poles and growth centres in regional planning – a review', *Environment and planning*, 1, pp 5–32.

ERICKSON, R. A. (1974) 'The regional impact of growth firms: The case of Boeing, 1963–1968', *Land economics*, 50, pp 127–136.

FLORENCE, P. S. (1948) *Investment location and size of plant*, Cambridge, University Press.

FLORENCE, P. S. (1961) *The logic of British and American industry*, revised edition, London, Routledge and Kegan Paul.

HÄGERSTRAND, T. (1965) 'Aspects of the spatial structure of social communication and the diffusion of information', *Papers, Regional Science Association*, 16, pp 27–42.

HAIG, R. M. (1926) 'Towards an understanding of the metropolis', *Quarterly Journal of Economics*, 40, pp 179–208, 402–434.

HIRSCHMAN, A. O. (1958) *The strategy of economic development*, New Haven, Yale University Press.

ISARD, W., SCHOOLER, E. W. and VIETORISZ, T. (1959) *Industrial complex analysis and regional development*, Cambridge, Massachusetts, M.I.T. Press.

ISARD, W. (1960) *Methods of regional analysis*, Cambridge, Massachusetts, M.I.T. Press.

ISARD, W. and LANGFORD, T. W. (1971) *Regional input-output study : recollections, reflections and diverse notes on the Philadelphia experience*, Cambridge, Massachusetts, M.I.T. Press.

KEEBLE, D. E. (1969) 'Local industrial linkage and manufacturing growth in outer London', *Town Planning Review*, 40, pp 163–188.

KEEBLE, D. E. (1971) 'Employment mobility in Britain', in M. Chisholm and G. Manners (eds) *Spatial policy problems of the British economy*, Cambridge, University Press.

LEONTIEF, W. W. (1951) *The structure of American economy 1919–1939*, New York, Oxford University Press.

LEONTIEF, W. W. *et al.* (1953) *Studies in the structure of the American economy*, New York, Oxford University Press.

MOORE, C. W. (1972) 'Industrial linkage development paths in growth poles: A research methodology', *Environment and planning*, 4, pp 253–271.

MYRDAL, G. (1963) *Economic theory and underdeveloped regions*, London, University Paperbacks, Methuen.

PERROUX, F. (1950) 'Economic space, theory and applications', *Quarterly Journal of Economics*, 64, pp 90–97.

PERROUX, F. (1964) 'La notion de pole de croissance', *L'économie du XXème siècle*, 2nd ed., Paris Presse Universitaire de France.

SIMON, H. A. (1957) *Models of Man*, New York, John Wiley.

TODD, D. (1974) 'An appraisal of the development pole concept in regional analysis', *Environment and planning*, 6, pp 291–306.

WOOD, P. A. (1969) 'Industrial location and linkage' *Area*, 1, pp 32–39.

ZELINSKY, W. (1962) 'Has American industry been decentralizing? The evidence for the 1939–54 period', *Economic Geography*, 38, pp 251–69.

Acknowledgements   Grateful acknowledgement is made to the following sources for material used in this unit:

Figure 1 and Table 3 from W. Isard, *Methods of Regional Analysis* by permission of the M.I.T. Press, Cambridge, Massachusetts; *Figure 2* from D. E. Keeble, 'Local industrial linkage and manufacturing growth in outer London' in *Town Planning Review*, 40:2, 1969; *Figure 3* from D. Todd, 'An appraisal of the development pole concept' in *Environment and Planning A*, 6 (3), 1974; *Table 4* from T. Hägerstrand, *Innovation Diffusion as a Spatial Process*, University of Chicago Press, translated from *Innovationsförloppet korologist synpunkt*, published by C. W. K. Gleerup, Lund, Sweden, 1953.

Block and Unit Titles

Block 1   **Regional Imbalance.**

Unit 1   An introductory framework.

Unit 2   Measures of regional imbalance – the case of the United Kingdom.

Block 2   **The Macro Approach – the analysis of regional change.**

Unit 3   The movement of goods between regions.

Unit 4   Export base theory and the growth and decline of regions.

Unit 5   Changing the region's role.

Unit 6   Regional growth and the movement of labour and capital.

Block 3   **The Micro Approach – economic and social surfaces.**

Unit 7   Economic and social surfaces.

Unit 8   The movement of firms.

Unit 9   Human migration.

Unit 10   The consequences of labour migration.

Unit 11   Economic complexes.

Block 4   **Government Intervention.**

Unit 12   Reasons for government intervention.

Unit 13   Methods of government intervention.

Unit 14   Economic planning in a developing country: Nigeria.

Unit 15   Economic planning in a mixed economy: United Kingdom.

Unit 16   Economic planning in a socialist country: Poland.

The Single Market Review

IMPACT ON COMPETITION
AND SCALE EFFECTS

COMPETITION ISSUES

The Single Market Review series

Subseries **I —** **Impact on manufacturing**
Volume: 1 Food, drink and tobacco processing machinery
2 Pharmaceutical products
3 Textiles and clothing
4 Construction site equipment
5 Chemicals
6 Motor vehicles
7 Processed foodstuffs
8 Telecommunications equipment

Subseries **II —** **Impact on services**
Volume: 1 Insurance
2 Air transport
3 Credit institutions and banking
4 Distribution
5 Road freight transport
6 Telecommunications: liberalized services
7 Advertising
8 Audio-visual services and production
9 Single information market
10 Single energy market
11 Transport networks

Subseries **III —** **Dismantling of barriers**
Volume: 1 Technical barriers to trade
2 Public procurement
3 Customs and fiscal formalities at frontiers
4 Industrial property rights
5 Capital market liberalization
6 Currency management costs

Subseries **IV —** **Impact on trade and investment**
Volume: 1 Foreign direct investment
2 Trade patterns inside the single market
3 Trade creation and trade diversion
4 External access to European markets

Subseries **V —** **Impact on competition and scale effects**
Volume: 1 Price competition and price convergence
2 Intangible investments
3 Competition issues
4 Economies of scale

Subseries **VI —** **Aggregate and regional impact**
Volume: 1 Regional growth and convergence
2 The cases of Greece, Spain, Ireland and Portugal
3 Trade, labour and capital flows: the less developed regions
4 Employment, trade and labour costs in manufacturing
5 Aggregate results of the single market programme

Results of the business survey